ISBN 0-8373-2260-X
C-2260 CAREER EXAMINATION SERIES

This is your PASSBOOK® for...

Campus Security Officer

Test Preparation Study Guide

Questions & Answers

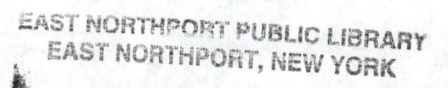

NLC
NATIONAL LEARNING CORPORATION

Copyright © 2014 by

National Learning Corporation
212 Michael Drive, Syosset, New York 11791

All rights reserved, including the right of reproduction in whole or in part, in any form or by any means, electronic or mechanical, including photocopying, recording, or by any information storage and retrieval system, without permission in writing from the Publisher.

(516) 921-8888
(800) 645-6337
FAX: (516) 921-8743
www.passbooks.com
sales @ passbooks.com
info @ passbooks.com

PRINTED IN THE UNITED STATES OF AMERICA

PASSBOOK®
NOTICE

This book is SOLELY intended for, is sold ONLY to, and its use is RESTRICTED to *individual*, bona fide applicants or candidates who qualify by virtue of having seriously filed applications for appropriate license, certificate, professional and/or promotional advancement, higher school matriculation, scholarship, or other legitimate requirements of educational and/or governmental authorities.

This book is NOT intended for use, class instruction, tutoring, training, duplication, copying, reprinting, excerption, or adaptation, etc., by:

(1) Other publishers

(2) Proprietors and/or Instructors of "Coaching" and/or Preparatory Courses

(3) Personnel and/or Training Divisions of commercial, industrial, and governmental organizations

(4) Schools, colleges, or universities and/or their departments and staffs, including teachers and other personnel

(5) Testing Agencies or Bureaus

(6) Study groups which seek by the purchase of a single volume to copy and/or duplicate and/or adapt this material for use by the group as a whole without having purchased individual volumes for each of the members of the group

(7) Et al.

Such persons would be in violation of appropriate Federal and State statutes.

PROVISION OF LICENSING AGREEMENTS. — Recognized educational commercial, industrial, and governmental institutions and organizations, and others legitimately engaged in educational pursuits, including training, testing, and measurement activities, may address a request for a licensing agreement to the copyright owners, who will determine whether, and under what conditions, including fees and charges, the materials in this book may be used by them. In other words, a licensing facility exists for the legitimate use of the material in this book on other than an individual basis. However, it is asseverated and affirmed here that the material in this book *CANNOT* be used without the receipt of the express permission of such a licensing agreement from the Publishers.

NATIONAL LEARNING CORPORATION
212 Michael Drive
Syosset, New York 11791

Inquiries re licensing agreements should be addressed to:
The President
National Learning Corporation
212 Michael Drive
Syosset, New York 11791

PASSBOOK SERIES®

THE *PASSBOOK SERIES®* has been created to prepare applicants and candidates for the ultimate academic battlefield – the examination room.

At some time in our lives, each and every one of us may be required to take an examination – for validation, matriculation, admission, qualification, registration, certification, or licensure.

Based on the assumption that every applicant or candidate has met the basic formal educational standards, has taken the required number of courses, and read the necessary texts, the *PASSBOOK SERIES®* furnishes the one special preparation which may assure passing with confidence, instead of failing with insecurity. Examination questions – together with answers – are furnished as the basic vehicle for study so that the mysteries of the examination and its compounding difficulties may be eliminated or diminished by a sure method.

This book is meant to help you pass your examination provided that you qualify and are serious in your objective.

The entire field is reviewed through the huge store of content information which is succinctly presented through a provocative and challenging approach – the question-and-answer method.

A climate of success is established by furnishing the correct answers at the end of each test.

You soon learn to recognize types of questions, forms of questions, and patterns of questioning. You may even begin to anticipate expected outcomes.

You perceive that many questions are repeated or adapted so that you can gain acute insights, which may enable you to score many sure points.

You learn how to confront new questions, or types of questions, and to attack them confidently and work out the correct answers.

You note objectives and emphases, and recognize pitfalls and dangers, so that you may make positive educational adjustments.

Moreover, you are kept fully informed in relation to new concepts, methods, practices, and directions in the field.

You discover that you are actually taking the examination all the time: you are preparing for the examination by "taking" an examination, not by reading extraneous and/or supererogatory textbooks.

In short, this PASSBOOK®, used directedly, should be an important factor in helping you to pass your test.

CAMPUS SECURITY OFFICER

DUTIES
Controls and directs traffic on campus roadways and parking lots; investigates complaints received personally or as assigned by supervisor; enforces traffic and parking regulations; summons local police, fire departments and ambulance services in cases of law violation, fire or other emergency; gives information and directions to students and vistors; operates radio telephone dispatching equipment; performs a variety of related tasks as required.

SUBJECT OF EXAMINATION
The written test will be designed to test for knowledge, skills, and/or abilities in such areas as:
1. Understanding and interpreting written material;
2. Applying written information in a security situation;
3. Evaluating information and evidence; and
4. Following directions (maps).

HOW TO TAKE A TEST

I. YOU MUST PASS AN EXAMINATION

A. WHAT EVERY CANDIDATE SHOULD KNOW

Examination applicants often ask us for help in preparing for the written test. What can I study in advance? What kinds of questions will be asked? How will the test be given? How will the papers be graded?

As an applicant for a civil service examination, you may be wondering about some of these things. Our purpose here is to suggest effective methods of advance study and to describe civil service examinations.

Your chances for success on this examination can be increased if you know how to prepare. Those "pre-examination jitters" can be reduced if you know what to expect. You can even experience an adventure in good citizenship if you know why civil service exams are given.

B. WHY ARE CIVIL SERVICE EXAMINATIONS GIVEN?

Civil service examinations are important to you in two ways. As a citizen, you want public jobs filled by employees who know how to do their work. As a job seeker, you want a fair chance to compete for that job on an equal footing with other candidates. The best-known means of accomplishing this two-fold goal is the competitive examination.

Exams are widely publicized throughout the nation. They may be administered for jobs in federal, state, city, municipal, town or village governments or agencies.

Any citizen may apply, with some limitations, such as the age or residence of applicants. Your experience and education may be reviewed to see whether you meet the requirements for the particular examination. When these requirements exist, they are reasonable and applied consistently to all applicants. Thus, a competitive examination may cause you some uneasiness now, but it is your privilege and safeguard.

C. HOW ARE CIVIL SERVICE EXAMS DEVELOPED?

Examinations are carefully written by trained technicians who are specialists in the field known as "psychological measurement," in consultation with recognized authorities in the field of work that the test will cover. These experts recommend the subject matter areas or skills to be tested; only those knowledges or skills important to your success on the job are included. The most reliable books and source materials available are used as references. Together, the experts and technicians judge the difficulty level of the questions.

Test technicians know how to phrase questions so that the problem is clearly stated. Their ethics do not permit "trick" or "catch" questions. Questions may have been tried out on sample groups, or subjected to statistical analysis, to determine their usefulness.

Written tests are often used in combination with performance tests, ratings of training and experience, and oral interviews. All of these measures combine to form the best-known means of finding the right person for the right job.

II. HOW TO PASS THE WRITTEN TEST

A. NATURE OF THE EXAMINATION

To prepare intelligently for civil service examinations, you should know how they differ from school examinations you have taken. In school you were assigned certain definite pages to read or subjects to cover. The examination questions were quite detailed and usually emphasized memory. Civil service exams, on the other hand, try to discover your present ability to perform the duties of a position, plus your potentiality to learn these duties. In other words, a civil service exam attempts to predict how successful you will be. Questions cover such a broad area that they cannot be as minute and detailed as school exam questions.

In the public service similar kinds of work, or positions, are grouped together in one "class." This process is known as *position-classification*. All the positions in a class are paid according to the salary range for that class. One class title covers all of these positions, and they are all tested by the same examination.

B. FOUR BASIC STEPS

1) Study the announcement

How, then, can you know what subjects to study? Our best answer is: "Learn as much as possible about the class of positions for which you've applied." The exam will test the knowledge, skills and abilities needed to do the work.

Your most valuable source of information about the position you want is the official exam announcement. This announcement lists the training and experience qualifications. Check these standards and apply only if you come reasonably close to meeting them.

The brief description of the position in the examination announcement offers some clues to the subjects which will be tested. Think about the job itself. Review the duties in your mind. Can you perform them, or are there some in which you are rusty? Fill in the blank spots in your preparation.

Many jurisdictions preview the written test in the exam announcement by including a section called "Knowledge and Abilities Required," "Scope of the Examination," or some similar heading. Here you will find out specifically what fields will be tested.

2) Review your own background

Once you learn in general what the position is all about, and what you need to know to do the work, ask yourself which subjects you already know fairly well and which need improvement. You may wonder whether to concentrate on improving your strong areas or on building some background in your fields of weakness. When the announcement has specified "some knowledge" or "considerable knowledge," or has used adjectives like "beginning principles of..." or "advanced ... methods," you can get a clue as to the number and difficulty of questions to be asked in any given field. More questions, and hence broader coverage, would be included for those subjects which are more important in the work. Now weigh your strengths and weaknesses against the job requirements and prepare accordingly.

3) Determine the level of the position

Another way to tell how intensively you should prepare is to understand the level of the job for which you are applying. Is it the entering level? In other words, is this the position in which beginners in a field of work are hired? Or is it an intermediate or advanced level? Sometimes this is indicated by such words as "Junior" or "Senior" in the class title. Other jurisdictions use Roman numerals to designate the level – Clerk I, Clerk II, for example. The word "Supervisor" sometimes appears in the title. If the level is not indicated by the title, check the description of duties. Will you be working under very close supervision, or will you have responsibility for independent decisions in this work?

4) Choose appropriate study materials

Now that you know the subjects to be examined and the relative amount of each subject to be covered, you can choose suitable study materials. For beginning level jobs, or even advanced ones, if you have a pronounced weakness in some aspect of your training, read a modern, standard textbook in that field. Be sure it is up to date and has general coverage. Such books are normally available at your library, and the librarian will be glad to help you locate one. For entry-level positions, questions of appropriate difficulty are chosen – neither highly advanced questions, nor those too simple. Such questions require careful thought but not advanced training.

If the position for which you are applying is technical or advanced, you will read more advanced, specialized material. If you are already familiar with the basic principles of your field, elementary textbooks would waste your time. Concentrate on advanced textbooks and technical periodicals. Think through the concepts and review difficult problems in your field.

These are all general sources. You can get more ideas on your own initiative, following these leads. For example, training manuals and publications of the government agency which employs workers in your field can be useful, particularly for technical and professional positions. A letter or visit to the government department involved may result in more specific study suggestions, and certainly will provide you with a more definite idea of the exact nature of the position you are seeking.

III. KINDS OF TESTS

Tests are used for purposes other than measuring knowledge and ability to perform specified duties. For some positions, it is equally important to test ability to make adjustments to new situations or to profit from training. In others, basic mental abilities not dependent on information are essential. Questions which test these things may not appear as pertinent to the duties of the position as those which test for knowledge and information. Yet they are often highly important parts of a fair examination. For very general questions, it is almost impossible to help you direct your study efforts. What we can do is to point out some of the more common of these general abilities needed in public service positions and describe some typical questions.

1) General information

Broad, general information has been found useful for predicting job success in some kinds of work. This is tested in a variety of ways, from vocabulary lists to questions about current events. Basic background in some field of work, such as sociology or economics, may be sampled in a group of questions. Often these are principles which have become familiar to most persons through exposure rather than through formal training. It is difficult to advise you how to study for these questions; being alert to the world around you is our best suggestion.

2) Verbal ability

An example of an ability needed in many positions is verbal or language ability. Verbal ability is, in brief, the ability to use and understand words. Vocabulary and grammar tests are typical measures of this ability. Reading comprehension or paragraph interpretation questions are common in many kinds of civil service tests. You are given a paragraph of written material and asked to find its central meaning.

3) Numerical ability

Number skills can be tested by the familiar arithmetic problem, by checking paired lists of numbers to see which are alike and which are different, or by interpreting charts and graphs. In the latter test, a graph may be printed in the test booklet which you are asked to use as the basis for answering questions.

4) Observation

A popular test for law-enforcement positions is the observation test. A picture is shown to you for several minutes, then taken away. Questions about the picture test your ability to observe both details and larger elements.

5) Following directions

In many positions in the public service, the employee must be able to carry out written instructions dependably and accurately. You may be given a chart with several columns, each column listing a variety of information. The questions require you to carry out directions involving the information given in the chart.

6) Skills and aptitudes

Performance tests effectively measure some manual skills and aptitudes. When the skill is one in which you are trained, such as typing or shorthand, you can practice. These tests are often very much like those given in business school or high school courses. For many of the other skills and aptitudes, however, no short-time preparation can be made. Skills and abilities natural to you or that you have developed throughout your lifetime are being tested.

Many of the general questions just described provide all the data needed to answer the questions and ask you to use your reasoning ability to find the answers. Your best preparation for these tests, as well as for tests of facts and ideas, is to be at your physical and mental best. You, no doubt, have your own methods of getting into an exam-taking mood and keeping "in shape." The next section lists some ideas on this subject.

IV. KINDS OF QUESTIONS

Only rarely is the "essay" question, which you answer in narrative form, used in civil service tests. Civil service tests are usually of the short-answer type. Full instructions for answering these questions will be given to you at the examination. But in case this is your first experience with short-answer questions and separate answer sheets, here is what you need to know:

1) Multiple-choice Questions

Most popular of the short-answer questions is the "multiple choice" or "best answer" question. It can be used, for example, to test for factual knowledge, ability to solve problems or judgment in meeting situations found at work.

A multiple-choice question is normally one of three types—
- It can begin with an incomplete statement followed by several possible endings. You are to find the one ending which *best* completes the statement, although some of the others may not be entirely wrong.
- It can also be a complete statement in the form of a question which is answered by choosing one of the statements listed.
- It can be in the form of a problem – again you select the best answer.

Here is an example of a multiple-choice question with a discussion which should give you some clues as to the method for choosing the right answer:

When an employee has a complaint about his assignment, the action which will *best* help him overcome his difficulty is to
   A. discuss his difficulty with his coworkers
   B. take the problem to the head of the organization
   C. take the problem to the person who gave him the assignment
   D. say nothing to anyone about his complaint

In answering this question, you should study each of the choices to find which is best. Consider choice "A" – Certainly an employee may discuss his complaint with fellow employees, but no change or improvement can result, and the complaint remains unresolved. Choice "B" is a poor choice since the head of the organization probably does not know what assignment you have been given, and taking your problem to him is known as "going over the head" of the supervisor. The supervisor, or person who made the assignment, is the person who can clarify it or correct any injustice. Choice "C" is, therefore, correct. To say nothing, as in choice "D," is unwise. Supervisors have and interest in knowing the problems employees are facing, and the employee is seeking a solution to his problem.

2) True/False Questions

The "true/false" or "right/wrong" form of question is sometimes used. Here a complete statement is given. Your job is to decide whether the statement is right or wrong.

SAMPLE: A person-to-person long-distance telephone call costs less than a station-to-station call to the same city.

This statement is wrong, or false, since person-to-person calls are more expensive.

This is not a complete list of all possible question forms, although most of the others are variations of these common types. You will always get complete directions for answering questions. Be sure you understand *how* to mark your answers – ask questions until you do.

V. RECORDING YOUR ANSWERS

For an examination with very few applicants, you may be told to record your answers in the test booklet itself. Separate answer sheets are much more common. If this separate answer sheet is to be scored by machine – and this is often the case – it is highly important that you mark your answers correctly in order to get credit.

An electric scoring machine is often used in civil service offices because of the speed with which papers can be scored. Machine-scored answer sheets must be marked with a pencil, which will be given to you. This pencil has a high graphite content which responds to the electric scoring machine. As a matter of fact, stray dots may register as answers, so do not let your pencil rest on the answer sheet while you are pondering the correct answer. Also, if your pencil lead breaks or is otherwise defective, ask for another.

Since the answer sheet will be dropped in a slot in the scoring machine, be careful not to bend the corners or get the paper crumpled.

The answer sheet normally has five vertical columns of numbers, with 30 numbers to a column. These numbers correspond to the question numbers in your test booklet. After each number, going across the page are four or five pairs of dotted lines. These short dotted lines have small letters or numbers above them. The first two pairs may also have a "T" or "F" above the letters. This indicates that the first two pairs only are to be used if the questions are of the true-false type. If the questions are multiple choice, disregard the "T" and "F" and pay attention only to the small letters or numbers.

Answer your questions in the manner of the sample that follows:

32. The largest city in the United States is
    A. Washington, D.C.
    B. New York City
    C. Chicago
    D. Detroit
    E. San Francisco

1) Choose the answer you think is best. (New York City is the largest, so "B" is correct.)
2) Find the row of dotted lines numbered the same as the question you are answering. (Find row number 32)
3) Find the pair of dotted lines corresponding to the answer. (Find the pair of lines under the mark "B.")
4) Make a solid black mark between the dotted lines.

VI. BEFORE THE TEST

Common sense will help you find procedures to follow to get ready for an examination. Too many of us, however, overlook these sensible measures. Indeed, nervousness and fatigue have been found to be the most serious reasons why applicants fail to do their best on civil service tests. Here is a list of reminders:

- Begin your preparation early – Don't wait until the last minute to go scurrying around for books and materials or to find out what the position is all about.
- Prepare continuously – An hour a night for a week is better than an all-night cram session. This has been definitely established. What is more, a night a

week for a month will return better dividends than crowding your study into a shorter period of time.
- Locate the place of the exam – You have been sent a notice telling you when and where to report for the examination. If the location is in a different town or otherwise unfamiliar to you, it would be well to inquire the best route and learn something about the building.
- Relax the night before the test – Allow your mind to rest. Do not study at all that night. Plan some mild recreation or diversion; then go to bed early and get a good night's sleep.
- Get up early enough to make a leisurely trip to the place for the test – This way unforeseen events, traffic snarls, unfamiliar buildings, etc. will not upset you.
- Dress comfortably – A written test is not a fashion show. You will be known by number and not by name, so wear something comfortable.
- Leave excess paraphernalia at home – Shopping bags and odd bundles will get in your way. You need bring only the items mentioned in the official notice you received; usually everything you need is provided. Do not bring reference books to the exam. They will only confuse those last minutes and be taken away from you when in the test room.
- Arrive somewhat ahead of time – If because of transportation schedules you must get there very early, bring a newspaper or magazine to take your mind off yourself while waiting.
- Locate the examination room – When you have found the proper room, you will be directed to the seat or part of the room where you will sit. Sometimes you are given a sheet of instructions to read while you are waiting. Do not fill out any forms until you are told to do so; just read them and be prepared.
- Relax and prepare to listen to the instructions
- If you have any physical problem that may keep you from doing your best, be sure to tell the test administrator. If you are sick or in poor health, you really cannot do your best on the exam. You can come back and take the test some other time.

VII. AT THE TEST

The day of the test is here and you have the test booklet in your hand. The temptation to get going is very strong. Caution! There is more to success than knowing the right answers. You must know how to identify your papers and understand variations in the type of short-answer question used in this particular examination. Follow these suggestions for maximum results from your efforts:

1) Cooperate with the monitor
The test administrator has a duty to create a situation in which you can be as much at ease as possible. He will give instructions, tell you when to begin, check to see that you are marking your answer sheet correctly, and so on. He is not there to guard you, although he will see that your competitors do not take unfair advantage. He wants to help you do your best.

2) Listen to all instructions
Don't jump the gun! Wait until you understand all directions. In most civil service tests you get more time than you need to answer the questions. So don't be in a hurry.

Read each word of instructions until you clearly understand the meaning. Study the examples, listen to all announcements and follow directions. Ask questions if you do not understand what to do.

3) Identify your papers

Civil service exams are usually identified by number only. You will be assigned a number; you must not put your name on your test papers. Be sure to copy your number correctly. Since more than one exam may be given, copy your exact examination title.

4) Plan your time

Unless you are told that a test is a "speed" or "rate of work" test, speed itself is usually not important. Time enough to answer all the questions will be provided, but this does not mean that you have all day. An overall time limit has been set. Divide the total time (in minutes) by the number of questions to determine the approximate time you have for each question.

5) Do not linger over difficult questions

If you come across a difficult question, mark it with a paper clip (useful to have along) and come back to it when you have been through the booklet. One caution if you do this – be sure to skip a number on your answer sheet as well. Check often to be sure that you have not lost your place and that you are marking in the row numbered the same as the question you are answering.

6) Read the questions

Be sure you know what the question asks! Many capable people are unsuccessful because they failed to *read* the questions correctly.

7) Answer all questions

Unless you have been instructed that a penalty will be deducted for incorrect answers, it is better to guess than to omit a question.

8) Speed tests

It is often better NOT to guess on speed tests. It has been found that on timed tests people are tempted to spend the last few seconds before time is called in marking answers at random – without even reading them – in the hope of picking up a few extra points. To discourage this practice, the instructions may warn you that your score will be "corrected" for guessing. That is, a penalty will be applied. The incorrect answers will be deducted from the correct ones, or some other penalty formula will be used.

9) Review your answers

If you finish before time is called, go back to the questions you guessed or omitted to give them further thought. Review other answers if you have time.

10) Return your test materials

If you are ready to leave before others have finished or time is called, take ALL your materials to the monitor and leave quietly. Never take any test material with you. The monitor can discover whose papers are not complete, and taking a test booklet may be grounds for disqualification.

VIII. EXAMINATION TECHNIQUES

1) Read the general instructions carefully. These are usually printed on the first page of the exam booklet. As a rule, these instructions refer to the timing of the examination; the fact that you should not start work until the signal and must stop work at a signal, etc. If there are any *special* instructions, such as a choice of questions to be answered, make sure that you note this instruction carefully.

2) When you are ready to start work on the examination, that is as soon as the signal has been given, read the instructions to each question booklet, underline any key words or phrases, such as *least, best, outline, describe* and the like. In this way you will tend to answer as requested rather than discover on reviewing your paper that you *listed without describing*, that you selected the *worst* choice rather than the *best* choice, etc.

3) If the examination is of the objective or multiple-choice type – that is, each question will also give a series of possible answers: A, B, C or D, and you are called upon to select the best answer and write the letter next to that answer on your answer paper – it is advisable to start answering each question in turn. There may be anywhere from 50 to 100 such questions in the three or four hours allotted and you can see how much time would be taken if you read through all the questions before beginning to answer any. Furthermore, if you come across a question or group of questions which you know would be difficult to answer, it would undoubtedly affect your handling of all the other questions.

4) If the examination is of the essay type and contains but a few questions, it is a moot point as to whether you should read all the questions before starting to answer any one. Of course, if you are given a choice – say five out of seven and the like – then it is essential to read all the questions so you can eliminate the two that are most difficult. If, however, you are asked to answer all the questions, there may be danger in trying to answer the easiest one first because you may find that you will spend too much time on it. The best technique is to answer the first question, then proceed to the second, etc.

5) Time your answers. Before the exam begins, write down the time it started, then add the time allowed for the examination and write down the time it must be completed, then divide the time available somewhat as follows:
   - If 3-1/2 hours are allowed, that would be 210 minutes. If you have 80 objective-type questions, that would be an average of 2-1/2 minutes per question. Allow yourself no more than 2 minutes per question, or a total of 160 minutes, which will permit about 50 minutes to review.
   - If for the time allotment of 210 minutes there are 7 essay questions to answer, that would average about 30 minutes a question. Give yourself only 25 minutes per question so that you have about 35 minutes to review.

6) The most important instruction is to *read each question* and make sure you know what is wanted. The second most important instruction is to *time yourself properly* so that you answer every question. The third most

important instruction is to *answer every question*. Guess if you have to but include something for each question. Remember that you will receive no credit for a blank and will probably receive some credit if you write something in answer to an essay question. If you guess a letter – say "B" for a multiple-choice question – you may have guessed right. If you leave a blank as an answer to a multiple-choice question, the examiners may respect your feelings but it will not add a point to your score. Some exams may penalize you for wrong answers, so in such cases *only*, you may not want to guess unless you have some basis for your answer.

7) Suggestions
   a. Objective-type questions
      1. Examine the question booklet for proper sequence of pages and questions
      2. Read all instructions carefully
      3. Skip any question which seems too difficult; return to it after all other questions have been answered
      4. Apportion your time properly; do not spend too much time on any single question or group of questions
      5. Note and underline key words – *all, most, fewest, least, best, worst, same, opposite,* etc.
      6. Pay particular attention to negatives
      7. Note unusual option, e.g., unduly long, short, complex, different or similar in content to the body of the question
      8. Observe the use of "hedging" words – *probably, may, most likely,* etc.
      9. Make sure that your answer is put next to the same number as the question
      10. Do not second-guess unless you have good reason to believe the second answer is definitely more correct
      11. Cross out original answer if you decide another answer is more accurate; do not erase until you are ready to hand your paper in
      12. Answer all questions; guess unless instructed otherwise
      13. Leave time for review

   b. Essay questions
      1. Read each question carefully
      2. Determine exactly what is wanted. Underline key words or phrases.
      3. Decide on outline or paragraph answer
      4. Include many different points and elements unless asked to develop any one or two points or elements
      5. Show impartiality by giving pros and cons unless directed to select one side only
      6. Make and write down any assumptions you find necessary to answer the questions
      7. Watch your English, grammar, punctuation and choice of words
      8. Time your answers; don't crowd material

8) Answering the essay question

Most essay questions can be answered by framing the specific response around several key words or ideas. Here are a few such key words or ideas:

M's: manpower, materials, methods, money, management

P's: purpose, program, policy, plan, procedure, practice, problems, pitfalls, personnel, public relations

   a. Six basic steps in handling problems:
1. Preliminary plan and background development
2. Collect information, data and facts
3. Analyze and interpret information, data and facts
4. Analyze and develop solutions as well as make recommendations
5. Prepare report and sell recommendations
6. Install recommendations and follow up effectiveness

   b. Pitfalls to avoid
1. *Taking things for granted* – A statement of the situation does not necessarily imply that each of the elements is necessarily true; for example, a complaint may be invalid and biased so that all that can be taken for granted is that a complaint has been registered
2. *Considering only one side of a situation* – Wherever possible, indicate several alternatives and then point out the reasons you selected the best one
3. *Failing to indicate follow up* – Whenever your answer indicates action on your part, make certain that you will take proper follow-up action to see how successful your recommendations, procedures or actions turn out to be
4. *Taking too long in answering any single question* – Remember to time your answers properly

IX. AFTER THE TEST

Scoring procedures differ in detail among civil service jurisdictions although the general principles are the same. Whether the papers are hand-scored or graded by machine we have described, they are nearly always graded by number. That is, the person who marks the paper knows only the number – never the name – of the applicant. Not until all the papers have been graded will they be matched with names. If other tests, such as training and experience or oral interview ratings have been given, scores will be combined. Different parts of the examination usually have different weights. For example, the written test might count 60 percent of the final grade, and a rating of training and experience 40 percent. In many jurisdictions, veterans will have a certain number of points added to their grades.

After the final grade has been determined, the names are placed in grade order and an eligible list is established. There are various methods for resolving ties between those who get the same final grade – probably the most common is to place first the name of the person whose application was received first. Job offers are made from the eligible list in the order the names appear on it. You will be notified of your grade and your rank as soon as all these computations have been made. This will be done as rapidly as possible.

People who are found to meet the requirements in the announcement are called "eligibles." Their names are put on a list of eligible candidates. An eligible's chances of getting a job depend on how high he stands on this list and how fast agencies are filling jobs from the list.

When a job is to be filled from a list of eligibles, the agency asks for the names of people on the list of eligibles for that job. When the civil service commission receives this request, it sends to the agency the names of the three people highest on this list. Or, if the job to be filled has specialized requirements, the office sends the agency the names of the top three persons who meet these requirements from the general list.

The appointing officer makes a choice from among the three people whose names were sent to him. If the selected person accepts the appointment, the names of the others are put back on the list to be considered for future openings.

That is the rule in hiring from all kinds of eligible lists, whether they are for typist, carpenter, chemist, or something else. For every vacancy, the appointing officer has his choice of any one of the top three eligibles on the list. This explains why the person whose name is on top of the list sometimes does not get an appointment when some of the persons lower on the list do. If the appointing officer chooses the second or third eligible, the No. 1 eligible does not get a job at once, but stays on the list until he is appointed or the list is terminated.

X. HOW TO PASS THE INTERVIEW TEST

The examination for which you applied requires an oral interview test. You have already taken the written test and you are now being called for the interview test – the final part of the formal examination.

You may think that it is not possible to prepare for an interview test and that there are no procedures to follow during an interview. Our purpose is to point out some things you can do in advance that will help you and some good rules to follow and pitfalls to avoid while you are being interviewed.

What is an interview supposed to test?

The written examination is designed to test the technical knowledge and competence of the candidate; the oral is designed to evaluate intangible qualities, not readily measured otherwise, and to establish a list showing the relative fitness of each candidate – as measured against his competitors – for the position sought. Scoring is not on the basis of "right" and "wrong," but on a sliding scale of values ranging from "not passable" to "outstanding." As a matter of fact, it is possible to achieve a relatively low score without a single "incorrect" answer because of evident weakness in the qualities being measured.

Occasionally, an examination may consist entirely of an oral test – either an individual or a group oral. In such cases, information is sought concerning the technical knowledges and abilities of the candidate, since there has been no written examination for this purpose. More commonly, however, an oral test is used to supplement a written examination.

Who conducts interviews?

The composition of oral boards varies among different jurisdictions. In nearly all, a representative of the personnel department serves as chairman. One of the members of the board may be a representative of the department in which the candidate would work. In some cases, "outside experts" are used, and, frequently, a businessman or some other representative of the general public is asked to serve. Labor and management or other special groups may be represented. The aim is to secure the services of experts in the appropriate field.

However the board is composed, it is a good idea (and not at all improper or unethical) to ascertain in advance of the interview who the members are and what groups they represent. When you are introduced to them, you will have some idea of their backgrounds and interests, and at least you will not stutter and stammer over their names.

What should be done before the interview?
While knowledge about the board members is useful and takes some of the surprise element out of the interview, there is other preparation which is more substantive. It *is* possible to prepare for an oral interview – in several ways:

1) Keep a copy of your application and review it carefully before the interview
This may be the only document before the oral board, and the starting point of the interview. Know what education and experience you have listed there, and the sequence and dates of all of it. Sometimes the board will ask you to review the highlights of your experience for them; you should not have to hem and haw doing it.

2) Study the class specification and the examination announcement
Usually, the oral board has one or both of these to guide them. The qualities, characteristics or knowledges required by the position sought are stated in these documents. They offer valuable clues as to the nature of the oral interview. For example, if the job involves supervisory responsibilities, the announcement will usually indicate that knowledge of modern supervisory methods and the qualifications of the candidate as a supervisor will be tested. If so, you can expect such questions, frequently in the form of a hypothetical situation which you are expected to solve. NEVER go into an oral without knowledge of the duties and responsibilities of the job you seek.

3) Think through each qualification required
Try to visualize the kind of questions you would ask if you were a board member. How well could you answer them? Try especially to appraise your own knowledge and background in each area, *measured against the job sought*, and identify any areas in which you are weak. Be critical and realistic – do not flatter yourself.

4) Do some general reading in areas in which you feel you may be weak
For example, if the job involves supervision and your past experience has NOT, some general reading in supervisory methods and practices, particularly in the field of human relations, might be useful. Do NOT study agency procedures or detailed manuals. The oral board will be testing your understanding and capacity, not your memory.

5) Get a good night's sleep and watch your general health and mental attitude
You will want a clear head at the interview. Take care of a cold or any other minor ailment, and of course, no hangovers.

What should be done on the day of the interview?
Now comes the day of the interview itself. Give yourself plenty of time to get there. Plan to arrive somewhat ahead of the scheduled time, particularly if your appointment is in the fore part of the day. If a previous candidate fails to appear, the board might be ready for you a bit early. By early afternoon an oral board is almost invariably behind schedule if there are many candidates, and you may have to wait.

Take along a book or magazine to read, or your application to review, but leave any extraneous material in the waiting room when you go in for your interview. In any event, relax and compose yourself.

The matter of dress is important. The board is forming impressions about you – from your experience, your manners, your attitude, and your appearance. Give your personal appearance careful attention. Dress your best, but not your flashiest. Choose conservative, appropriate clothing, and be sure it is immaculate. This is a business interview, and your appearance should indicate that you regard it as such. Besides, being well groomed and properly dressed will help boost your confidence.

Sooner or later, someone will call your name and escort you into the interview room. *This is it.* From here on you are on your own. It is too late for any more preparation. But remember, you asked for this opportunity to prove your fitness, and you are here because your request was granted.

What happens when you go in?

The usual sequence of events will be as follows: The clerk (who is often the board stenographer) will introduce you to the chairman of the oral board, who will introduce you to the other members of the board. Acknowledge the introductions before you sit down. Do not be surprised if you find a microphone facing you or a stenotypist sitting by. Oral interviews are usually recorded in the event of an appeal or other review.

Usually the chairman of the board will open the interview by reviewing the highlights of your education and work experience from your application – primarily for the benefit of the other members of the board, as well as to get the material into the record. Do not interrupt or comment unless there is an error or significant misinterpretation; if that is the case, do not hesitate. But do not quibble about insignificant matters. Also, he will usually ask you some question about your education, experience or your present job – partly to get you to start talking and to establish the interviewing "rapport." He may start the actual questioning, or turn it over to one of the other members. Frequently, each member undertakes the questioning on a particular area, one in which he is perhaps most competent, so you can expect each member to participate in the examination. Because time is limited, you may also expect some rather abrupt switches in the direction the questioning takes, so do not be upset by it. Normally, a board member will not pursue a single line of questioning unless he discovers a particular strength or weakness.

After each member has participated, the chairman will usually ask whether any member has any further questions, then will ask you if you have anything you wish to add. Unless you are expecting this question, it may floor you. Worse, it may start you off on an extended, extemporaneous speech. The board is not usually seeking more information. The question is principally to offer you a last opportunity to present further qualifications or to indicate that you have nothing to add. So, if you feel that a significant qualification or characteristic has been overlooked, it is proper to point it out in a sentence or so. Do not compliment the board on the thoroughness of their examination – they have been sketchy, and you know it. If you wish, merely say, "No thank you, I have nothing further to add." This is a point where you can "talk yourself out" of a good impression or fail to present an important bit of information. Remember, *you close the interview yourself.*

The chairman will then say, "That is all, Mr. _____, thank you." Do not be startled; the interview is over, and quicker than you think. Thank him, gather your belongings and take your leave. Save your sigh of relief for the other side of the door.

How to put your best foot forward

Throughout this entire process, you may feel that the board individually and collectively is trying to pierce your defenses, seek out your hidden weaknesses and embarrass and confuse you. Actually, this is not true. They are obliged to make an appraisal of your qualifications for the job you are seeking, and they want to see you in your best light. Remember, they must interview all candidates and a non-cooperative candidate may become a failure in spite of their best efforts to bring out his qualifications. Here are 15 suggestions that will help you:

1) Be natural – Keep your attitude confident, not cocky

If you are not confident that you can do the job, do not expect the board to be. Do not apologize for your weaknesses, try to bring out your strong points. The board is interested in a positive, not negative, presentation. Cockiness will antagonize any board member and make him wonder if you are covering up a weakness by a false show of strength.

2) Get comfortable, but don't lounge or sprawl

Sit erectly but not stiffly. A careless posture may lead the board to conclude that you are careless in other things, or at least that you are not impressed by the importance of the occasion. Either conclusion is natural, even if incorrect. Do not fuss with your clothing, a pencil or an ashtray. Your hands may occasionally be useful to emphasize a point; do not let them become a point of distraction.

3) Do not wisecrack or make small talk

This is a serious situation, and your attitude should show that you consider it as such. Further, the time of the board is limited – they do not want to waste it, and neither should you.

4) Do not exaggerate your experience or abilities

In the first place, from information in the application or other interviews and sources, the board may know more about you than you think. Secondly, you probably will not get away with it. An experienced board is rather adept at spotting such a situation, so do not take the chance.

5) If you know a board member, do not make a point of it, yet do not hide it

Certainly you are not fooling him, and probably not the other members of the board. Do not try to take advantage of your acquaintanceship – it will probably do you little good.

6) Do not dominate the interview

Let the board do that. They will give you the clues – do not assume that you have to do all the talking. Realize that the board has a number of questions to ask you, and do not try to take up all the interview time by showing off your extensive knowledge of the answer to the first one.

7) Be attentive

You only have 20 minutes or so, and you should keep your attention at its sharpest throughout. When a member is addressing a problem or question to you, give him your undivided attention. Address your reply principally to him, but do not exclude the other board members.

8) Do not interrupt

A board member may be stating a problem for you to analyze. He will ask you a question when the time comes. Let him state the problem, and wait for the question.

9) Make sure you understand the question

Do not try to answer until you are sure what the question is. If it is not clear, restate it in your own words or ask the board member to clarify it for you. However, do not haggle about minor elements.

10) Reply promptly but not hastily

A common entry on oral board rating sheets is "candidate responded readily," or "candidate hesitated in replies." Respond as promptly and quickly as you can, but do not jump to a hasty, ill-considered answer.

11) Do not be peremptory in your answers

A brief answer is proper – but do not fire your answer back. That is a losing game from your point of view. The board member can probably ask questions much faster than you can answer them.

12) Do not try to create the answer you think the board member wants

He is interested in what kind of mind you have and how it works – not in playing games. Furthermore, he can usually spot this practice and will actually grade you down on it.

13) Do not switch sides in your reply merely to agree with a board member

Frequently, a member will take a contrary position merely to draw you out and to see if you are willing and able to defend your point of view. Do not start a debate, yet do not surrender a good position. If a position is worth taking, it is worth defending.

14) Do not be afraid to admit an error in judgment if you are shown to be wrong

The board knows that you are forced to reply without any opportunity for careful consideration. Your answer may be demonstrably wrong. If so, admit it and get on with the interview.

15) Do not dwell at length on your present job

The opening question may relate to your present assignment. Answer the question but do not go into an extended discussion. You are being examined for a *new* job, not your present one. As a matter of fact, try to phrase ALL your answers in terms of the job for which you are being examined.

Basis of Rating

Probably you will forget most of these "do's" and "don'ts" when you walk into the oral interview room. Even remembering them all will not ensure you a passing grade. Perhaps you did not have the qualifications in the first place. But remembering them will help you to put your best foot forward, without treading on the toes of the board members.

Rumor and popular opinion to the contrary notwithstanding, an oral board wants you to make the best appearance possible. They know you are under pressure – but they also want to see how you respond to it as a guide to what your reaction would be under the pressures of the job you seek. They will be influenced by the degree of poise you display, the personal traits you show and the manner in which you respond.

EXAMINATION SECTION

EXAMINATION SECTION
TEST 1

DIRECTIONS: Each question or incomplete statement is followed by several suggested answers or completions. Select the one that BEST answers the question or completes the statement. *PRINT THE LETTER OF THE CORRECT ANSWER IN THE SPACE AT THE RIGHT.*

1. As a general rule, which of the following areas on a campus would be most in need of protection by a physical barrier?
   Areas

   A. set aside for group activities
   B. smaller than 40 feet in diameter
   C. with roof access
   D. less than 18 feet above ground

   1._____

2. For a campus officer to be armed, it is customary for him to complete a signed statement pledging himself to certain guidelines. Which of the following would typically be included in such a statement?
   I. The firearm will never be used as a club or similar weapon.
   II. Before shooting directly at a person, the officer will fire at least one warning shot.
   III. The firearm is only to be drawn when the officer's life, or the life of another, is threatened.
   IV. Shots directed at a perpetrator should be intended to disable, rather than kill.
   The CORRECT answer is:

   A. I, III
   B. I, III, IV
   C. III *only*
   D. II, III, IV

   2._____

3. An arrest that is made after the security officer sees the offense committed is known as an arrest on

   A. reasonable suspicion of probable cause
   B. view
   C. detention
   D. complaint

   3._____

4. The gate valve alarm of a sprinkler system has sounded. This means that the

   A. sprinkler system has been activated
   B. main water riser to the valve has been shut off
   C. storage water level has dropped below minimum requirements
   D. secondary water valve has been closed

   4._____

5. A *dry* fire — from burning wood, paper, or textiles — is classified as Class

   A. A
   B. B
   C. C
   D. D

   5._____

2 (#1)

6. The main DISADVANTAGE associated with the use of local alarms in security systems is that

   A. sometimes nobody is around to hear them
   B. they are dependent on electrical power
   C. they must be placed in multiple locations
   D. they don't deter criminals from breaking and entering

7. Each of the following is a symptom exhibited by *huffers* of vapors produced by glue, gasoline, paint, or other substances EXCEPT

   A. slurred speech   B. violent behavior
   C. coughing   D. increased appetite

8. Legally, a theft from the inside of a vehicle that has been locked and entered unlawfully is called

   A. robbery   B. grand larceny
   C. burglary   D. petty larceny

9. Security problems that may be caused by severe heat include

   A. increased likelihood of loss of power
   B. electrical overheating
   C. greater ability for people to hide stolen property
   D. increased likelihood of fires

10. Which of the following campus features does the most to necessitate a 24-hour radio dispatcher?
    A

    A. residential community
    B. contractual installation such as food service
    C. valuable collection
    D. high-rise building or buildings

11. If rounds clocks are used by an officer on patrol,

    A. the clock areas should be evenly spaced
    B. each clock must be punched on every round, regardless of the order
    C. the clock locations should never be changed
    D. they should be punched in exactly the same order each time

12. Because of the operating costs involved, a _____ alarm system is used primarily for government-owned facilities.

    A. remote   B. central station
    C. local   D. proprietary station

13. When assisting victims at the scene of an accident, an officer may
    I. give nonprescription medication
    II. restrain a person who is having a seizure
    III. treat a victim for shock
    IV. give the person fluids if the person is conscious
    The CORRECT answer is:

    A. I only   B. II only   C. III, IV   D. IV only

14. When a(n) _____ is NOT generally an occasion on which a person, automobile, or premises may be legally searched.

    A. subject is being held for questioning
    B. warrant has been obtained
    C. emergency situation exists
    D. lawful arrest has been made

15. After a crime has been committed, a(n) _____ makes the most useful interview subject.

    A. witness   B. victim   C. suspect   D. informant

16. A _____ lock generally offers the LEAST amount of security.

    A. combination   B. pin tumbler
    C. disc tumbler   D. cipher

17. Evacuation guidelines for most campus buildings provide for an area warden, stair guard, and a group leader who is appointed from among the building's management personnel. Typically, a group leader will be responsible for controlling and directing about _____ people, depending on the floor size and layout.

    A. 5   B. 15   C. 25   D. 35

18. The campus has just received a bomb threat, and a search is underway. When searching individual rooms, an officer should begin

    A. at the door and move in a circular path
    B. at the corners and move inward
    C. with the furniture and then check the fixtures
    D. at the ceiling and move to the floor

19. The highest percentage of crime on school campuses typically occurs in

    A. classrooms and private offices
    B. residence hall or dorms
    C. parking lots
    D. commercial installations such as bookstores and food service

20. For most security applications, a report listing the holder of keys must be filed

    A. twice daily   B. daily
    C. twice weekly   D. weekly

21. The best driving speed for vehicle patrol services is generally between _____ miles per hour.

    A. 5-10   B. 15-20   C. 25-30   D. 35-40

22. Which of the following statements is generally FALSE?

    A. An officer should never approach a group of people without requesting backup, even if it is not needed.
    B. The officer should never draw a weapon as a tactic for discouraging violence.
    C. An officer should never confront hostile persons alone.
    D. When using a flashlight, the officer should hold it sheltered close to his body.

23. In general, security personnel may make an arrest if they
    I. observe a suspect taking property
    II. know a felony has been committed but did not see it happen
    III. know a misdemeanor has been committed but did not see it happen
    The CORRECT answer is:

    A. I only   B. I, II   C. I, III   D. II, III

24. Which of the following may be a visible symptom of the abuse of opiates such as morphine, codeine, or heroin?

    A. Antisocial behavior
    B. Constricted eye functions
    C. Pale, sweaty skin
    D. Rapid speech

25. A security officer is the first to arrive at the scene of an accident that has caused injury. The victim has an open wound that is bleeding dark red, in a steady stream. After taking precautions against blood-borne disease, the officer should

    A. flush the wound with water
    B. apply a tourniquet
    C. apply antiseptic
    D. apply direct pressure to the wound

26. When approaching a subject for a weapons search, the officer should inform the subject that the search is to be conducted

    A. after the subject has been apprehended
    B. from behind, with one hand placed on the subject's shoulder
    C. from the patrol car, through a bullhorn or intercom
    D. from a safe distance of at least five feet

27. Which of the following elements should be included in a shift report?
    I. Detailed accounts of reported incidents
    II. Time and number of patrol rounds completed
    III. Information on condition of lighting
    IV. Weather conditions
    The CORRECT answer is:

    A. I only
    B. II, III, IV
    C. III, IV
    D. I, II

28. A(n) _____ internal alarm would probably be most effective in protecting a safe or vault.

    A. audio
    B. ultrasonic
    C. photoelectric
    D. capacitance

29. A call has come in from a passenger on a stranded elevator to the switchboard operator. After the operator receives the relevant information, security and maintenance personnel are contacted. Security personnel should report to the

    A. floor where the elevator is stranded
    B. maintenance personnel for direction
    C. bottom floor
    D. top floor

30. The post indicator alarm of a sprinkler system has sounded. This means the   30.____

    A. sprinkler system has been activated
    B. main water riser to the valve has been shut off
    C. storage water level has dropped below minimum requirements
    D. secondary water valve has been closed

31. The primary goal of a private security officer at the scene of a recent crime is   31.____

    A. containment   B. witness interviews
    C. suspect apprehension   D. evidence gathering

32. If a security officer encounters an accident victim who has gone into shock, the officer   32.____
    should do each of the following EXCEPT

    A. keep the victim warm
    B. raise the victim's head
    C. treat injuries
    D. loosen the victim's clothing

33. For a security officer, the foundation of good report writing is considered to be   33.____

    A. through patrolling   B. good interviewing
    C. field note taking   D. outlining skills

34. The fundamental difference between a crime called *malicious destruction of property* and   34.____
    one called *vandalism* is one of

    A. jurisdiction
    B. apparent motive
    C. the monetary amount of damage
    D. the type of property that was damaged

35. The most commonly used form of access control in setting such as college campuses is   35.____

    A. cipher locks   B. compartmentalization
    C. flood lighting   D. entry gate posts

36. The _____ should be allowed input into the decision to arm security personnel for spe-   36.____
    cific situations or events.
        I.   employers of security personnel
        II. public
        III. security agency
        IV. local law enforcement agency
    The CORRECT answer is:

    A. I, III   B. I, IV
    C. II, III, IV   D. II, IV

37. Which of the following activities generally offers the greatest degree of flexibility in the   37.____
    delivery of security services?

    A. Report writing   B. Vehicle patrol
    C. Access control   D. Foot patrol

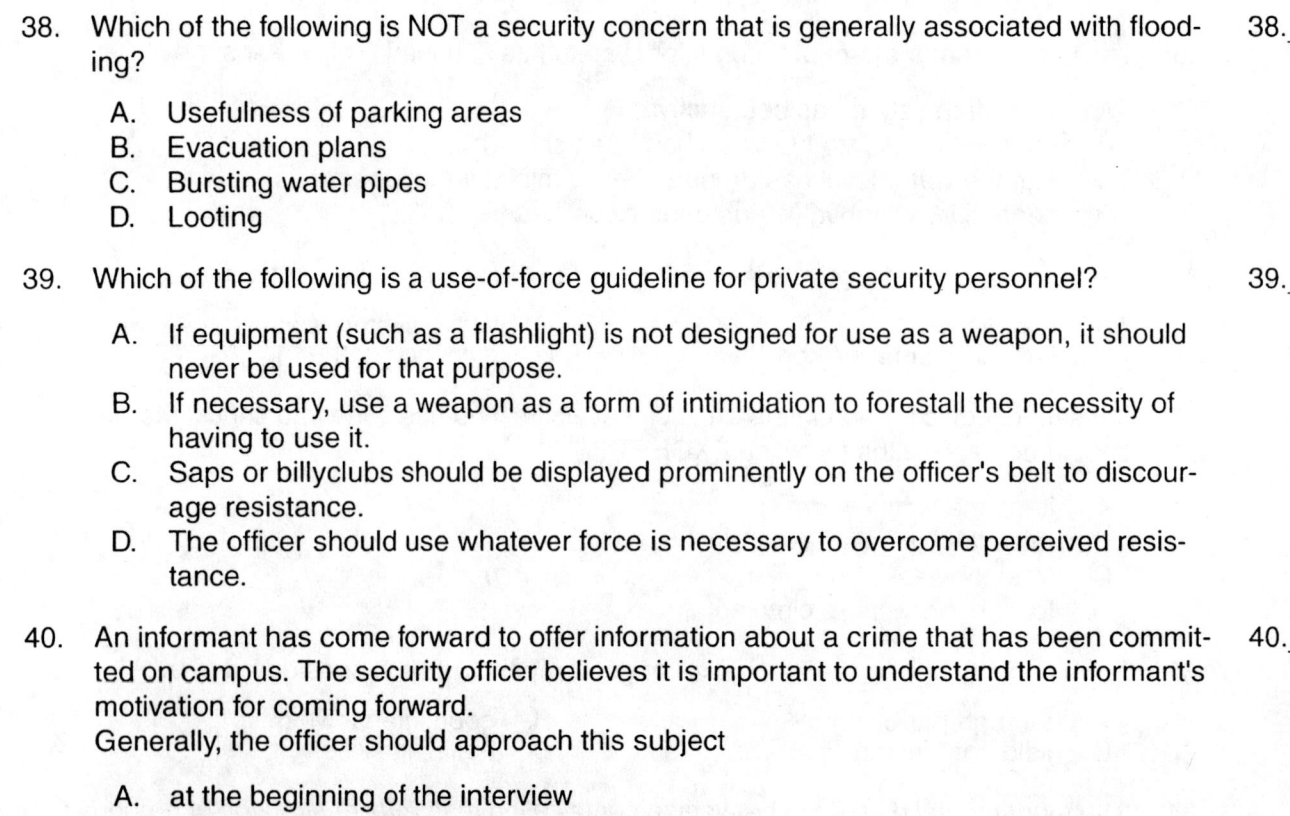

38. Which of the following is NOT a security concern that is generally associated with flooding?

   A. Usefulness of parking areas
   B. Evacuation plans
   C. Bursting water pipes
   D. Looting

39. Which of the following is a use-of-force guideline for private security personnel?

   A. If equipment (such as a flashlight) is not designed for use as a weapon, it should never be used for that purpose.
   B. If necessary, use a weapon as a form of intimidation to forestall the necessity of having to use it.
   C. Saps or billyclubs should be displayed prominently on the officer's belt to discourage resistance.
   D. The officer should use whatever force is necessary to overcome perceived resistance.

40. An informant has come forward to offer information about a crime that has been committed on campus. The security officer believes it is important to understand the informant's motivation for coming forward.
   Generally, the officer should approach this subject

   A. at the beginning of the interview
   B. when the informant least expects it
   C. after the informant has given an account, but before the officer has asked any questions
   D. at the conclusion of the interview

KEY (CORRECT ANSWERS)

1.	D	11.	A	21.	B	31.	A
2.	A	12.	A	22.	D	32.	B
3.	B	13.	C	23.	B	33.	C
4.	D	14.	A	24.	B	34.	B
5.	A	15.	A	25.	D	35.	D
6.	A	16.	C	26.	D	36.	A
7.	D	17.	B	27.	B	37.	B
8.	C	18.	A	28.	D	38.	C
9.	D	19.	B	29.	A	39.	A
10.	A	20.	B	30.	B	40.	D

TEST 2

DIRECTIONS: Each question or incomplete statement is followed by several suggested answers or completions. Select the one that BEST answers the question or completes the statement. *PRINT THE LETTER OF THE CORRECT ANSWER IN THE SPACE AT THE RIGHT.*

1. The campus has just received a bomb threat, and a search is underway. When searching individual rooms, team members should be instructed to

    A. start the search in the center of the room and move outward from there
    B. search slowly, first searching the area from the floor to waist height
    C. place a marker on any suspicious looking item
    D. enter a room completely before beginning the search

    1.____

2. When on a foot patrol assignment, an officer should

    A. turn the lights off whenever leaving a building
    B. stick to the shadows and avoid being seen
    C. observe the area to be patrolled before entering
    D. stick to the same pattern of patrolling

    2.____

3. Chemical fires are classified as Class

    A. A   B. B   C. C   D. D

    3.____

4. If campus security officers are to be armed, a _____ is typically most appropriate for their use.

    A. shotgun
    B. short-nosed .38-caliber revolver
    C. carbine
    D. long-nosed .357 magnum

    4.____

5. Which of the following is NOT a guideline that should be followed by security personnel who are on foot patrol at night?

    A. Avoid being lit from the back
    B. View the area to be patrolled in advance, if possible
    C. When entering buildings and are moving from room to room, open doors as quietly as possible
    D. Keep the flashlight on thumb pressure only

    5.____

6. Which of the following types of locks is most likely to be used with cabinets and desks?

    A. Combination lock   B. Disc tumbler lock
    C. Padlock   D. Cipher lock

    6.____

7. When on patrol, security personnel have an obligation to report
    I. traffic patterns
    II. improper employee conduct
    III. observed hazards
    IV. poor housekeeping or maintenance practices

    The CORRECT answer is:

    A. I only   B. II, IV
    C. II, III, IV   D. III, IV

    7.____

8. Towing policies for the enforcement of campus parking should include each of the following EXCEPT

   A. a contractual arrangement with a tow truck operator
   B. fines returnable to the local municipality, if possible
   C. the presence of a security officer at each towing incident
   D. a random pattern of towing that includes first-time offenders

9. Which of the following statements is generally TRUE?

   A. An officer should always display his badge prominently, especially when on night patrol.
   B. An officer should communicate with a dispatcher or other officers constantly while on duty.
   C. When approaching a vehicle, an officer should walk directly in front of the vehicle headlights.
   D. If a door has a window, an officer should look through it and examine the room before entering.

10. Which of the following is a sign that might be exhibited by a person who is on amphetamines or *uppers*?

    A. Loss of appetite
    B. Constricted pupils
    C. Rapid speech
    D. Uncontrolled laughing

11. Whenever possible, security policy guidelines for campus residence halls should include each of the following EXCEPT

    A. a periphery of high-intensity light around the exterior
    B. the use of interchangeable-core locking cylinders
    C. the use of only one main ground-floor entrance per building
    D. planting shrubs/trees outside first-floor rooms

12. An alarm system whose monitors are located in the main guard office is known as a _____ alarm system.

    A. remote
    B. central station
    C. local
    D. proprietary station

13. A security officer comes across a victim who has been badly burned. The officer should

    A. treat the victim for shock
    B. bandage the burn
    C. apply cold water to the burn
    D. apply an ointment or salve

14. Which of the following interview subjects typically presents a security officer with the least amount of difficulty?
    A(n)

    A. witness
    B. victim
    C. suspect
    D. informant

15. Access control to any campus will be ineffective in any case if _____ are not provided.

    A. physical barriers
    B. weapons
    C. floodlights
    D. secure locks

16. Generally, security personnel may detain a person if
    I. it is known that the subject has information regarding a crime
    II. there is probable cause to believe the person has unlawfully taken property that can be recovered by holding the person for a reasonable period of time
    III. it is suspected that the person will commit a crime in the near future
    The CORRECT answer is:

    A. I, II B. II only C. III only D. I, III

17. In general, departmental record control should place a _____ day limit on the time allotted for the removal of files from the office by security personnel.

    A. 1 B. 2-3 C. 5-7 D. 10-15

18. Keys to gates, buildings, and other secured equipment must generally be issued and returned by officers

    A. every day
    B. every week
    C. every month
    D. annually

19. A crime has just been committed and a security officer is the first to arrive at the scene. Before the police arrive, a handful of campus officials arrive and request to enter the crime scene.
    The best way to handle this is to

    A. keep them out by any means necessary
    B. request their cooperation in remaining outside the scene until the police have arrived
    C. refer them to the security supervisor
    D. defer to their wishes

20. Which of the following phrases has a different meaning from the others?

    A. Incident report
    B. Post journal
    C. Shift report
    D. Post log

21. In order to be effective, combination locks used for access control should have AT LEAST _____ numbers.

    A. 3 B. 4 C. 5 D. 6

22. The simplest, most effective, and trouble-free peripheral alarm system for low-risk applications would probably involve

    A. magnetic switches
    B. button switches
    C. metallic foil tape
    D. audio switches

23. During a bomb search, a suspicious-looking package is found. Security personnel should

    A. move the package to a secure location
    B. place the package in water
    C. prevent anyone from touching the package
    D. place a tag on the package

24. When assisting a victim at the scene of an accident, an officer may
    I. describe an injury to the victim
    II. lift an injured person to a sitting position
    III. try to remove a foreign object from the victim's eye
    IV. attempt to keep the victim warm
    The CORRECT answer is:

    A. I only   B. II, III   C. IV only   D. III, IV

25. Each of the following is a symptom of shock EXCEPT

    A. slow pulse
    B. intense thirst
    C. dilated pupils
    D. irregular breathing

26. When on vehicle patrol, an officer should

    A. park directly in front of the building to be inspected
    B. observe from a distance or in a drive-by before driving into an area
    C. use spotlights to meet inspection requirements
    D. keep all windows closed while driving

27. Which of the following is a guideline to be followed by security personnel who are required to testify in court?

    A. Avoid asking attorneys to repeat their questions
    B. Never use the phrase *I think*
    C. Answer all questions as completely as possible
    D. Avoid looking directly at the judge or jury

28. Of the following types of arrest, the one that is most troublesome for security officers to justify is one that is made on

    A. reasonable suspicion of probable cause
    B. view
    C. detention
    D. complaint

29. The primary DISADVANTAGE associated with the use of central station alarm monitors is that

    A. time is lost from the time the signal is received until personnel arrive at the alarm area
    B. they do not provide a link to outside law enforcement agencies
    C. intruders are tipped off that the alarm has been activated
    D. they do not pin down the exact location of the alarm site

30. When writing any report, a security officer should

    A. write in the third person
    B. make sure there is at least one copy made
    C. use a formal outline
    D. use as few words as possible

31. Generally, campus property such as audio-visual equipment and office machinery should be inventoried at LEAST

    A. monthly
    B. quarterly
    C. annually
    D. every two years

32. Security personnel who carry firearms should generally be required to requalify themselves at a firing range every

    A. 4 months   B. 6 months   C. year   D. two years

33. Which of the following campus building areas is generally LEAST likely to be used for the placement of a bomb?

    A. Elevator shafts
    B. Toilets
    C. Roofs
    D. Electrical panels

34. If padlocks are used in security systems, it is recommended that they be made of

    A. aluminum
    B. case-hardened steel
    C. cast iron
    D. hardened steel

35. An officer should make certain assumptions about foot patrol assignments. Which of the following is NOT one of these?

    A. Some form of communication is available for the officer to obtain assistance or request instructions.
    B. Most foot patrol assignments are single-officer duties.
    C. Only buildings that are open for public access will be included in the assignment.
    D. Back-up officers are available but are at some distance.

36. Which of the following statements about security personnel arrests is/are generally TRUE?
    I. The subject does not have to be under control in order for there to be an arrest.
    II. Detaining a person is a technical arrest.
    III. An arrest is made with the arresting persons identifying themselves and make a statement such as *you are under arrest,* and either touch the suspect or the suspect agrees.
    IV. The authority for the arrest must be known by the suspect.
    The CORRECT answer is:

    A. I, II, IV
    B. II, III, IV
    C. III, IV
    D. I, III

37. As a general rule, an area that is less than _____ from another structure should be protected by a physical barrier.

    A. 14 feet   B. 25 feet   C. 64 feet   D. 100 yards

38. Security concerns associated with extreme cold include each of the following EXCEPT

    A. delayed communication
    B. physical danger from frozen surfaces
    C. increased opportunity for concealing objects under clothes
    D. integrity of plumbing systems

39. Fires from flammable liquids or grease are classified as Class

    A. A   B. B   C. C   D. D

40. When interviewing the victim of a crime, which of the following is a guideline that should generally be followed by a security officer?
    A. Make sure at least one other officer is present.
    B. Maintain a calm, steady demeanor.
    C. Get the facts by any means necessary.
    D. Keep the victim away from others who are familiar to him/her.

KEY (CORRECT ANSWERS)

1. B	11. D	21. B	31. C
2. C	12. D	22. A	32. A
3. D	13. A	23. C	33. C
4. B	14. D	24. C	34. D
5. C	15. A	25. A	35. C
6. B	16. B	26. B	36. B
7. C	17. B	27. B	37. A
8. D	18. A	28. A	38. A
9. B	19. B	29. A	39. B
10. C	20. A	30. B	40. B

EXAMINATION SECTION
TEST 1

DIRECTIONS: Questions 1 through 5 are to be answered on the basis of the information, instructions, and sample question given below. Each question contains a GENERAL RULE, EXCEPTIONS, a PROBLEM, and the ACTION actually taken.

The GENERAL RULE explains what the special officer (security officer) should or should not do.

The EXCEPTIONS describe circumstances under which a special officer (security officer) should take action contrary to the GENERAL RULE.

However, an unusual emergency may justify taking an action that is not covered either by the GENERAL RULE or by the stated EXCEPTIONS.

The PROBLEM describes a situation requiring some action by the special officer (security officer).

ACTION describes what a special officer (security officer) actually did in that particular case.

Read carefully the GENERAL RULE and EXCEPTIONS, the PROBLEM, and the ACTION, and the mark A, B, C, or D in the space at the right in accordance with the following instructions:

  I. If an action is clearly justified under the general rule, mark your answer A.
  II. If an action is not justified under the general rule, but is justified under a stated exception, mark your answer B.
  III. If an action is not justified either by the general rule or by a stated exception, but does seem strongly justified by an unusual emergency situation, mark your answer C.
  IV. If an action does not seem justified for any of these reasons, mark your answer D.

SAMPLE QUESTION:

GENERAL RULE: A special officer (security officer) is not empowered to stop a person and search him for hidden weapons.
EXCEPTION: He may stop a person and search him if he has good reason to believe that he may be carrying a hidden weapon. Good reasons to believe he may be carrying a hidden weapon include (a) notification through official channels that a person may be armed, (b) a statement directly to the special officer (security officer) by the person himself that he is armed, and (c) the special officer's (security officer's) own direct observation.

PROBLEM: A special officer (security officer) on duty at a hospital clinic is notified by a woman patient at the clinic that a man sitting near her is making muttered threats that he has a gun and is going to shoot his doctor if the doctor gives him any trouble. Although the woman is upset, she seems to be telling the truth, and two other waiting patients con-

firm this. However, the special officer (security officer) approaches the man and sees no sign of a hidden weapon. The man tells the officer that he has no weapon.
ACTION: The special officer (security officer) takes the man aside into an empty office and proceeds to frisk him for a concealed weapon.

ANSWER: The answer cannot be A, because the general rule is that a special officer (security officer) is not empowered to search a person for hidden weapons. The answer cannot be B, because the notification did not come through official channels, the man did not tell the special officer (security officer) that he had a weapon, and the special officer (security officer) did not observe any weapon. However, since three people have confirmed that the man has said he has a weapon and is threatening to use it, this is pretty clearly an emergency situation that calls for action. Therefore, the answer is C.

1. GENERAL RULE: A special officer (security officer) on duty at a certain entrance is not to leave his post unguarded at any time.
EXCEPTION: He may leave the post for a brief period if he first summons a replacement. He may also leave if it is necessary for him to take prompt emergency action to prevent injury to persons or property.
PROBLEM: The special officer (security officer) sees a man running down a hall with a piece of iron pipe in his hand, chasing another man who is shouting for help. By going in immediate pursuit, there is a good chance that the special officer (security officer) can stop the man with the pipe.
ACTION: The special officer (security officer) leaves his post unguarded and pursues the man.

   The CORRECT answer is:

   A. IB. IIC. IIID. IV

2. GENERAL RULE: Special officers (security officers) assigned to a college campus are instructed not to arrest students for minor violations such as disorderly conduct; instead, the violation should be stopped and the incident should be reported to the college authorities, who will take disciplinary action.
EXCEPTION: A special officer (security officer) may arrest a student or take other appropriate action if failure to do so is likely to result in personal injury or property damage, or disruption of school activities, or if the incident involves serious criminal behavior.
PROBLEM: A special officer (security officer) is on duty in a college building where evening classes are being held. He is told that two students are causing a disturbance in a classroom. He arrives and finds that a fist fight is in progress and the classroom is in an uproar. The special officer (security officer) separates the two students who are fighting and takes them out of the room. Both of them seem to be intoxicated. They both have valid student ID cards.
ACTION: The special officer (security officer) takes down their names and addresses for his report, then tells them to leave the building with a warning not to return this evening.

   The CORRECT answer is:

   A. IB. IIC. IIID. IV

3. **GENERAL RULE**: A special officer (security officer) is not permitted to carry a gun while on duty.
EXCEPTION: A special officer (security officer) who disarms a person must keep the weapon in his possession for the brief period before he can turn it over to the proper authorities. A special officer (security officer) who is NOT on duty may, like any other citizen, own and carry a gun if he has a proper permit from the Police Department.
PROBLEM: A special officer (security officer) is assigned to a post where there have been a series of violent incidents in the past few days. He feels that these incidents could have been controlled much more easily if the people involved had seen that the special officer (security officer) had a gun. He has a gun at home, for which he has a valid permit.
ACTION: The special officer (security officer) brings his gun when he goes on duty. He does not plan to use it, but just show people that he has it so that they will not start any trouble.

The CORRECT answer is:

A. I   B. II   C. III   D. IV

4. **GENERAL RULE**: No one except a licensed physician or someone acting directly under a physician's orders may legally administer medicine to another person.
EXCEPTION: In a first aid situation, the special officer (security officer) is allowed to help a person suffering frori a heart condition or other disease to take medicine which the person has in his possession, provided that the person is conscious and requests this assistance.
PROBLEM: A special officer (security officer) on duty at a public building is told that a man has collapsed in the elevator. When the special officer (security officer) arrives at the scene, the man is barely conscious. He cannot speak, but he points to his pocket. The special officer (security officer) finds a pill bottle that says *one capsule in ease of need*. The man nods.
ACTION: The special officer (security officer) puts one capsule in the man's hand and guides the man's hand to his mouth.

The CORRECT answer is:

A. I   B. II   C. III   D. IV

5. **GENERAL RULE**: In case of a fire drill or fire alarm, special officers (security officers) on patrol in a building are to remain in their assigned areas to assist in the evacuation of persons from the building and to make sure that no one takes advantage of the situation by stealing property that is left unguarded.
EXCEPTION: Should there be an actual fire, special officers (security officers) will follow whatever instructions are given by the firefighters or police officers who arrive on the scene to take charge.
PROBLEM: A special officer (security officer) is on duty patroling the fifth floor of a building when a fire alarm sounds. The fire is in a supply closet at one end of the fifth floor. All personnel have been evacuated from the floor. Neither police nor firemen have yet shown up.
ACTION: The special officer (security officer) stays on the fifth floor at a safe distance from the supply closet.

The CORRECT answer is:

A. I   B. II   C. III   D. IV

KEY (CORRECT ANSWERS)

1. B
2. A
3. D
4. B
5. A

EXAMINATION SECTION

TEST 1

DIRECTIONS: Each question or incomplete statement is followed by several suggested answers or completions. Select the one that BEST answers the question or completes the statement. *PRINT THE LETTER OF THE CORRECT ANSWER IN THE SPACE AT THE RIGHT.*

Questions 1-4.

DIRECTIONS: Questions 1 through 4 are based on the picture entitled *Contents of a Woman's Handbag*. Assume that all of the contents are shown in the picture.

CONTENTS OF A WOMAN'S HANDBAG

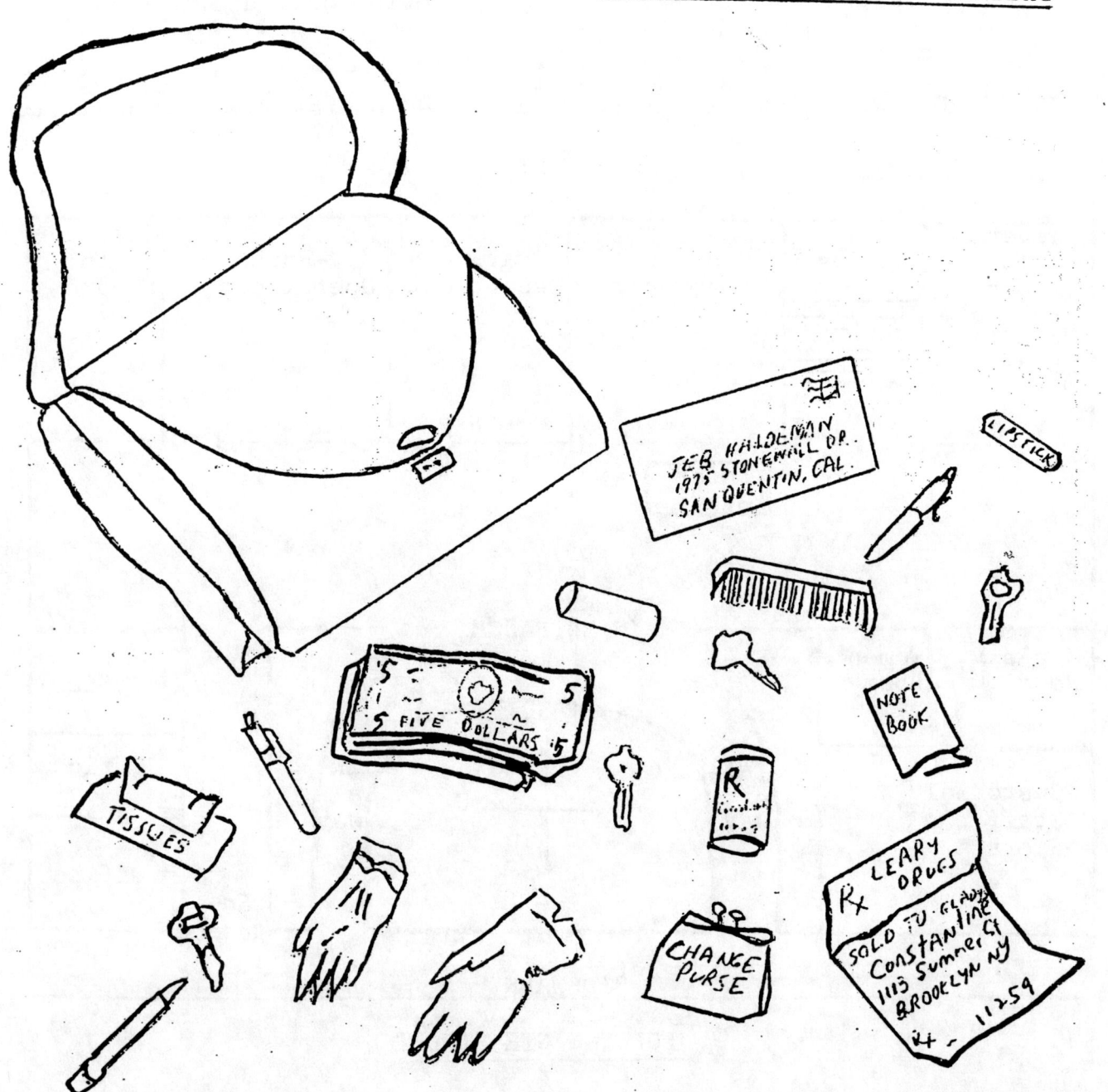

1. Where does Gladys Constantine live?
    A. Chalmers Street in Manhattan
    B. Summer Street in Manhattan
    C. Summer Street in Brooklyn
    D. Chalmers Street in Brooklyn

2. How many keys were in the handbag?
    A. 2   B. 3   C. 4   D. 5

3. How much money was in the handbag? _____ dollar(s).
    A. Exactly five   B. More than five
    C. Exactly ten   D. Less than one

4. The sales slip found in the handbag shows the purchase of which of the following?
    A. The handbag   B. Lipstick
    C. Tissues   D. Prescription medicine

Questions 5-8.

DIRECTIONS: Questions 5 through 8 are based on the floor plan below.

FLOOR PLAN

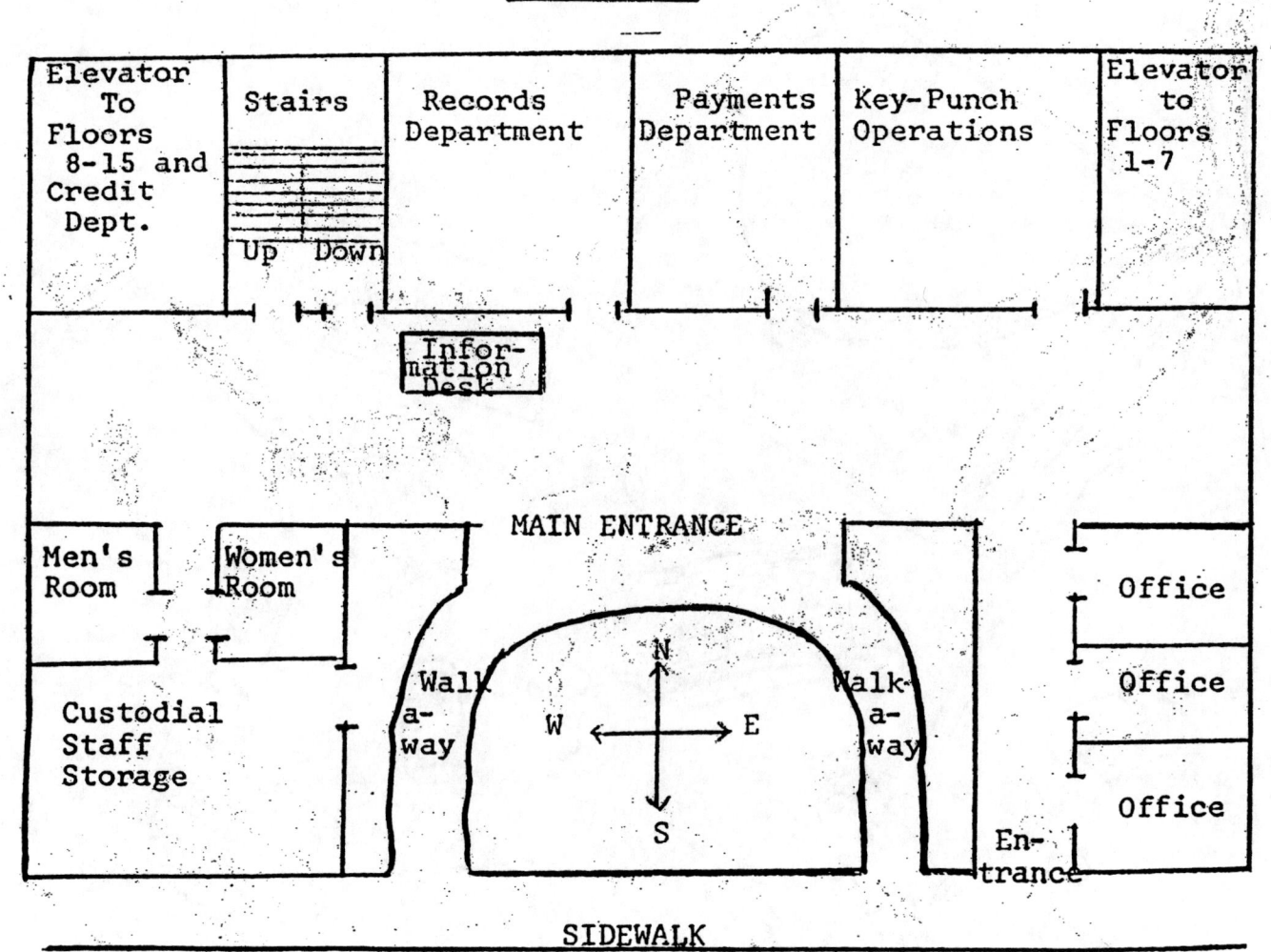

3 (#1)

5. A special officer (security officer) on duty at the main entrance must be aware of other outside entrances to his area of the building. These unguarded entrances are usually kept locked, but they are important in case of fire or other emergency.
Besides the main entrance, how many OTHER entrances shown on the floor plan directly face Forty-ninth Street? ____ other entrances.
   A. No   B. One   C. Two   D. Three

6. A person who arrives at the main entrance and asks to be directed to the Credit Department SHOULD be told to
   A. take the elevator on the left
   B. take the elevator on the right
   C. go to a different entrance
   D. go up the stairs on the left

7. On the east side of the entrance can be found
   A. a storage room   B. offices
   C. toilets   D. stairs

8. The space DIRECTLY BEHIND the Information Desk in the floor plan is occupied by
   A. up and down stairs   B. key punch operations
   C. toilets   D. the records department

Questions 9-12.

DIRECTIONS: Answer Questions 9 to 12 on the basis of the information given in the passage below.

The public often believes that the main job of a uniformed officer is to enforce laws by simply arresting people. In reality, however, many of the situations that an officer deals with do not call for the use of his arrest power. In the first place, an officer spends much of his time preventing crimes from happening, by spotting potential violations or suspicious behavior and taking action to prevent illegal acts. In the second place, many of the situations in which officers are called on for assistance involve elements like personal arguments, husband-wife quarrels, noisy juveniles, or mentally disturbed persons. The majority of these problems do not result in arrests and convictions, and often they do not even involve illegal behavior. In the third place, even in situations where there seems to be good reason to make an arrest, an officer may have to exercise very good judgment. There are times when making an arrest too soon could touch off a riot, or could result in the detention of a minor offender while major offenders escaped, or could cut short the gathering of necessary on-the-scene evidence.

9. The above passage IMPLIES that most citizens
   A. will start to riot if they see an arrest being made
   B. appreciate the work that law enforcement officers do
   C. do not realize that making arrests is only a small part of law enforcement
   D. never call for assistance unless they are involved in a personal argument or a husband-wife quarrel

10. According to the passage, one way in which law enforcement officers can prevent crimes from happening is by
    A. arresting suspicious characters
    B. letting minor offenders go free
    C. taking action on potential violations
    D. refusing to get involved in husband-wife fights

11. According to the passage, which of the following statements is NOT true of situations involving mentally disturbed persons?
    A. It is a waste of time to call on law enforcement officers for assistance in such situations.
    B. Such situations may not involve illegal behavior
    C. Such situations often do not result in arrests.
    D. Citizens often turn to law enforcement officers for help in such situations.

12. The last sentence in the passage mentions *detention of minor offenders*.
    Of the following, which BEST explains the meaning of the word *detention* as used here?
    A. Sentencing someone
    B. Indicting someone
    C. Calling someone before a grand jury
    D. Arresting someone

Questions 13-28.

DIRECTIONS: In answering Questions 13 through 28, assume that *you* means a special officer (security officer) on duty. Your basic responsibilities are safeguarding people and property and maintaining order in the area to which you are assigned. You are in uniform, and you are not armed. You keep in touch with your supervisory station either by telephone or by a two-way radio (walkie-talkie).

13. It is a general rule that if the security alarm goes off showing that someone has made an unlawful entrance into a building, no officer responsible for security shall proceed to investigate alone. Each officer must be accompanied by at least one other officer.
    Of the following, which is the MOST probable reason for this rule?
    A. It is dangerous for an officer to investigate such a situation alone.
    B. The intruder might try to bribe an officer to let him go.
    C. One officer may be inexperienced and needs an experienced partner.
    D. Two officers are better than one officer in writing a report of the investigation.

14. You are on weekend duty on the main floor of a public building. The building is closed to the public on weekends, but some employees are sometimes asked to work weekends. You have been instructed to use cautious good judgment in opening the door for such persons.
Of the following, which one MOST clearly shows the poorest judgment?
   A. Admitting an employee who is personally known to you without asking to see any identification except the permit slip signed by the employee's supervisor
   B. Refusing to admit someone whom you do not recognize but who claims left his identification at home
   C. Admitting to the building only those who can give a detailed description of their weekend work duties
   D. Leaving the entrance door locked for a while to make regulation security checks of other areas in the building with the result that no one can either enter or leave during these periods

15. You are on duty at a public building. An office employee tells you that she left her purse in her desk when she went out to lunch, and she has just discovered that it is gone. She has been back from lunch for half an hour and has not left her desk during this period.
What should you do FIRST?
   A. Warn all security personnel to stop any suspicious-looking person who is seen with a purse
   B. Ask for a description of the purse
   C. Call the Lost and Found and ask if a purse has been turned in
   D. Obtain statements from any employees who were in the office during the lunch hour

16. You are patrolling your assigned area in a public building. You hear a sudden crash and the sound of running footsteps. You investigate and find that someone has forced open a locked entrance to the building.
What is the FIRST thing you should do?
   A. Close the door and try to fix the lock so that no one else can get in
   B. Use your two-way radio to report the emergency and summon help
   C. Chase after the person whose running footsteps you heard
   D. Go immediately to your base office and make out a brief written report

17. You and another special officer (security officer) are on duty in the main waiting area at a welfare center. A caseworker calls both of you over and whispers that one of the clients, Richard Roe, may be carrying a gun.
Of the following, what is the BEST action for both of you to take?
   A. You should approach the man, one on each side, and one of you should say loudly and clearly, "Richard Roe, you are under arrest."

  B. Both of you should ask the man to go with you to a private room, and then find out if he is carrying a gun
  C. Both of you should grab him, handcuff him, and take him to the nearest precinct station house
  D. Both of you should watch him carefully but not do anything unless he actually pulls a gun

18. You are on duty at a welfare center. You are told that a caseworker is being threatened by a man with a knife. You go immediately to the scene, and you find the caseworker lying on the floor with blood spurting from a wound in his arm. You do not know who the attacker is. What should you do FIRST?
  A. Ask the caseworker for a description of the attacker so that you can set out in pursuit and try to catch him
  B. Take down the names and addresses of any witnesses to the incident
  C. Give first aid to the caseworker, if you can, and immediately call for an ambulance
  D. Search the people standing around in the room for the knife

19. As a special officer (security officer), you have been patrolling a special section of a hospital building for a week. Smoking is not allowed in this section because the oxygen tanks in use here could easily explode. However, you have observed that some employees sneak into the linen-supply room in this section in order to smoke without anybody seeing them.
Of the following, which is the BEST way for you to deal with this situation?
  A. Whenever you catch anyone smoking, call his supervisor immediately
  B. Request the Building Superintendent to put a padlock on the door of the linen-supply room
  C. Ignore the smoking because you do not want to get a reputation for interfering in the private affairs of other employees
  D. Report the situation to your supervisor and follow his instructions

20. You are on duty at a hospital. You have been assigned to guard the main door, and you are responsible for remaining at your post until relieved. On one of the wards for which you are not responsible, there is a patient who was wounded in a street fight. This patient is under arrest for killing another man in this fight, and he is supposed to be under round-the-clock police guard. A nurse tells you that one of the police officers assigned to guard the patient has suddenly taken ill and has to periodically leave his post to go to the washroom. The nurse is worried because she thinks the patient might try to escape.
Of the following, which is the BEST action for you to take?

A. Tell the nurse to call you whenever the police officer leaves his post so that you can keep an eye on the patient while the officer is gone
B. Assume that the police officer probably knows his job, and that there is no reason for you to worry
C. Alert your supervisor to the nurse's report
D. Warn the police officer that the nurse has been talking about him

21. You are on night duty at a hospital where you are responsible for patrolling a large section of the main building. Your supervisor tells you that there have been several nighttime thefts from a supply room in your section and asks you to be especially alert for suspicious activity near this supply room.
Of the following, which is the MOST reasonable way to carry out your supervisor's direction?
    A. Check the supply room regularly at half-hour intervals
    B. Make frequent checks of the supply room at irregular intervals
    C. Station yourself by the door of the supply room and stay at this post all night
    D. Find a hidden spot from which you can watch the supply room and stay there all night

22. You are on duty at a vehicle entrance to a hospital. Parking space on the hospital grounds is strictly limited, and no one is ever allowed to park there unless they have an official parking permit. You have just stopped a driver who does not have a parking permit, but he explains that he is a doctor and he has a patient in the hospital.
What should you do?
    A. Let him park since he has explained that he is a doctor
    B. Ask in a friendly way, "*Can I check your identification?*"
    C. Call the Information Desk to make sure there is such a patient in the hospital
    D. Tell the driver politely but firmly that he will have to park somewhere else

23. You are on duty at a public building. A man was just mugged on a stairway. The mugger took the man's wallet and started to run down the stairs but tripped and fell. Now the mugger is lying unconscious at the bottom of the stairs and bleeding from the mouth.
The FIRST thing you should do is to
    A. search him to see if he is carrying any other stolen property
    B. pick him up and carry him away from the stairs
    C. try and revive him for questioning
    D. put in a call for an ambulance and police assistance

24. After someone breaks into an employee's locker at a public building, you interview the employee to determine what is missing from the locker. The employee becomes hysterical and asks why you are *wasting time with all these questions* instead of going after the thief.
The MOST reasonable thing for you to do is
   A. tell the employee that it is very important to have an accurate description of the missing articles
   B. quietly tell the employee to calm down and stop interfering with your work
   C. explain to the employee that you are only doing what you were told to do and that you don't make the rules
   D. assure the employee that there are a lot of people working on the case and that someone else is probably arresting the thief right now

25. You are on duty at a public building. An employee reports that a man has just held her up and taken her money. The employee says that the man was about 25 years old, with short blond hair and a pale complexion and was wearing blue jeans.
Of the following additional facts, which one would probably be MOST valuable to officers searching the building for the suspect?
   A. The man was wearing dark glasses.
   B. He had on a green jacket.
   C. He was about 5 feet 8 inches tall.
   D. His hands and fingernails were very dirty.

26. When the fire alarm goes off, it is your job as a special officer (security officer) to see that all employees leave the building quickly by the correct exits. A fire alarm has just sounded, and you are checking the offices on one of the floors. A supervisor in one office tells you, *"This is probably just another fire drill. I've sent my office staff out, but I don't want to stop my own work."*
What should you do?
   A. Insist politely but firmly that the supervisor must obey the fire rules.
   B. Tell the supervisor that it is all right this time but that the rules must be followed in the future.
   C. Tell the supervisor that he is under arrest.
   D. Allow the supervisor to do as he sees fit since he is in charge of his own office.

27. You are on duty on the main floor of a public building. You have been informed that a briefcase has just been stolen from an office on the tenth floor. You see a man getting off the elevator with a briefcase that matches the description of the one that was stolen.
What is the FIRST action you should take?
   A. Arrest the man and take him to the nearest public station
   B. Stop the man and say politely that you want to take a look at the briefcase

C. Take the briefcase from the man and tell him that he cannot have it back unless he can prove that it is his
D. Do not stop the man but note down his description and the exact time he got off the elevator

28. You are on duty at a welfare center. You have been told that two clients are arguing with a caseworker and making loud threats. You go to the scene, but the caseworker tells you that everything is now under control. The two clients, who are both mean-looking characters, are still there but seem to be acting normally.
What SHOULD you do?
    A. Apologize for having made a mistake and go away.
    B. Arrest the two men for having caused a disturbance.
    C. Insist on standing by until the interview is over, then escort the two men from the building.
    D. Leave the immediate scene but watch for any further developments.

29. You are on duty at a welfare center. A client comes up to you and says that two men just threatened him with a knife and made him give them his money. The client has alcohol on his breath and he is shabbily dressed. He points out the two men he says took the money.
Of the following, which is the BEST action to take?
    A. Arrest the two men on the client's complaint.
    B. Ignore the client's complaint since he doesn't look as if he could have had any money.
    C. Suggest to the client that he may be imagining things.
    D. Investigate and find out what happened.

Questions 30-35.

DIRECTIONS: Answer Questions 30 through 35 on the basis of the information given in the passage below. Assume that all questions refer to the same state described in the passage.

The courts and the police consider an "offense" as any conduct that is punishable by a fine or imprisonment. Such offenses include many kinds of acts - from behavior that is merely annoying, like throwing a noisy party that keeps everyone awake, all the way up to violent acts like murder. The law classifies offenses according to the penalties that are provided for them. In one state, minor offenses are called "violations." A violation is punishable by a fine of not more than $250 or imprisonment of not more than 15 days, or both. The annoying behavior mentioned above is an example of a violation. More serious offenses are classified as "crimes." Crimes are classified by the kind of penalty that is provided. A "misdemeanor" is a crime that is punishable by a fine of not more than $1,000 or by imprisonment of not more than one year, or both. Examples of misdemeanors include stealing something with a value of $100 or less, turning in a false alarm, or illegally possessing less than 1/8 of an ounce of a dangerous drug. A "felony" is a criminal offense punishable by imprisonment of more than one year. Murder is clearly a felony.

30. According to the above passage, any act that is punishable by imprisonment or by a fine is called a(n)
    A. offense   B. violation   C. crime   D. felony

31. According to the above passage, which of the following is classified as a crime?
    A. Offense punishable by 15 days imprisonment
    B. Minor offense
    C. Violation
    D. Misdemeanor

32. According to the above passage, if a person guilty of burglary can receive a prison sentence of 7 years or more, burglary would be classified as a
    A. violation   B. misdemeanor
    C. felony   D. violent act

33. According to the above passage, two offenses that would BOTH be classified as misdemeanors are
    A. making unreasonable noise and stealing a $90 bicycle
    B. stealing a $75 radio and possessing 1/16 of an ounce of heroin
    C. holding up a bank and possessing 1/4 of a pound of marijuana
    D. falsely reporting a fire and illegally double-parking

34. The above passage says that offenses are classified according to the penalties provided for them.
    On the basis of clues in the passage, who probably decides what the maximum penalties should be for the different kinds of offenses?
    A. The State lawmakers   B. The City police
    C. The Mayor   D. Officials in Washington, D.C.

35. Of the following, which BEST describes the subject matter of the passage?
    A. How society deals with criminals
    B. How offenses are classified
    C. Three types of criminal behavior
    D. The police approach to offenders

KEY (CORRECT ANSWERS)

1. C	11. A	21. B	31. D
2. C	12. D	22. D	32. C
3. B	13. A	23. D	33. B
4. D	14. C	24. A	34. A
5. B	15. B	25. C	35. B
6. A	16. B	26. A	
7. B	17. B	27. B	
8. D	18. C	28. D	
9. C	19. D	29. D	
10. C	20. C	30. A	

TEST 2

DIRECTIONS: Each question or incomplete statement is followed by several suggested answers or completions. Select the one that BEST answers the question or completes the statement. *PRINT THE LETTER OF THE CORRECT ANSWER IN THE SPACE AT THE RIGHT.*

Questions 1-5.

DIRECTIONS: Questions 1 through 5 are based on the drawing below showing a view of a waiting area in a public building.

1. A desk is shown in the drawing.
    Which of the following is on the desk? A(n)
    A. plant   B. telephone
    C. In-Out file   D. *Information* sign

2. On which floor is the waiting area?
    A. Basement   B. Main floor
    C. Second floor   D. Third floor

3. The door IMMEDIATELY TO THE RIGHT of the desk is a(n)
    A. door to the Personnel Office
    B. elevator door
    C. door to another corridor
    D. door to the stairs

4. Among the magazines on the tables in the waiting area are
    A. TIME and NEWSWEEK
    B. READER'S DIGEST and T.V. GUIDE
    C. NEW YORK and READER'S DIGEST
    D. TIME and T.V. GUIDE

5. One door is partly open. This is the door to
    A. the Director's office
    B. the Personnel Manager's office
    C. the stairs
    D. an unmarked office

Questions 6-9.

DIRECTIONS: Questions 6 through 9 are based on the drawing below showing the contents of a male suspect's pockets.

CONTENTS OF A MALE SUSPECT'S POCKETS

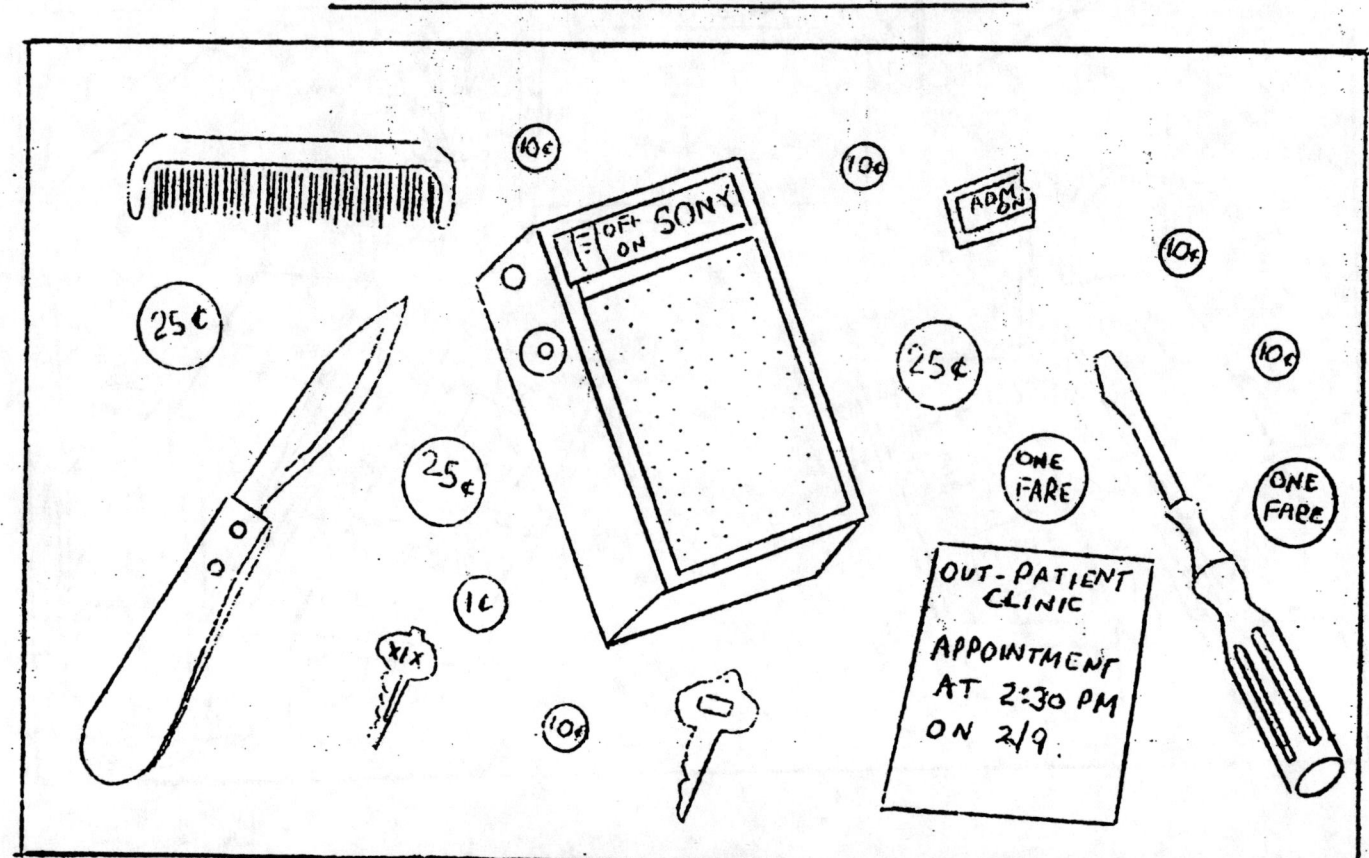

6. The suspect had a slip in his pockets showing an appointment at an out-patient clinic on
   A. February 9
   B. September 2
   C. February 19
   D. September 12

7. The transistor radio that was found on the suspect was made by
   A. RCA   B. GE   C. Sony   D. Zenith

8. The coins found in the suspect's pockets have a TOTAL value of
   A. 56¢   B. 77¢   C. $1.05   D. $1.26

9. All except one of the following were found in the suspect's pockets. Which was NOT found?   A
   A. ticket stub
   B. comb
   C. subway token
   D. pen

Questions 10-18.

DIRECTIONS: In answering Questions 10 through 18, assume that *you* means a special officer (security officer) on duty. Your basic responsibilities are safeguarding people and property and maintaining order in the area to which you are assigned. You are in uniform, and you are not armed. You keep in touch with your supervisory station either by telephone or by a two-way radio (a walkie-talkie).

10. You are on duty at a center run by the Department of Social Services. Two teenaged boys are on their way out of the center. As they go past you, they look at you and laugh, and one makes a remark to you in Spanish. You do not understand Spanish, but you suspect it was a nasty remark.
    What SHOULD you do?
    A. Give the boys a lecture about showing respect for a uniform.
    B. Tell the boys that they had better stay away from the center from now on.
    C. Call for an interpreter and insist that the boy repeat the remark to the interpreter.
    D. Let the boys go on their way since they have done nothing requiring your intervention.

11. You are on duty at a shelter run by the Department of Social Services. You know that many of the shelter clients have drinking problems, drug problems, or mental health problems. You get a call for assistance from a caseworker who says a fight has broken out. When you arrive on the scene, you see that about a dozen clients are engaged in a free-for-all and that two or three of them have pulled knives.
    The BEST course of action is to
    A. call for additional assistance and order all bystanders away from the area

B. jump into the center of the fighting group and try to separate the fighters
C. pick up a heavy object and start swinging at anybody who has a knife
D. try to find out what clients started the fight and place them under arrest

12. You have been assigned to duty at a children's shelter run by the Department of Social Services. The children range in age from 6 to 15, and many of them are at the shelter because they have no homes to go to.
Of the following, which is the BEST attitude for you to take in dealing with these youngsters?
    A. Assume that they admire and respect anyone in uniform and that they will not usually give you much trouble
    B. Assume that they fear and distrust anyone in uniform and that they are going to give you a hard time unless you act tough
    C. Expect that many of them are going to become juvenile delinquents because of their bad backgrounds and that you should be suspicious of everything they do
    D. Expect that many of them may be emotionally upset and that you should be alert for unusual behavior

13. You are on duty outside the emergency room of a hospital. You notice that an old man has been sitting on a bench outside the room for a long time. He arrived alone, and he has not spoken to anyone at all.
What SHOULD you do?
    A. Pay no attention to him since he is not bothering anyone.
    B. Tell him to leave since he does not seem to have any business there.
    C. Ask him if you can help him in any way.
    D. Do not speak to him, but keep an eye on him.

14. You are patrolling a section of a public building. An elderly woman carrying a heavy shopping bag asks you if you would watch the shopping bag for her while she keeps an appointment in the building.
What SHOULD you do?
    A. Watch the shopping bag for her since her appointment probably will not take long.
    B. Refuse her request, explaining that your duties keep you on the move.
    C. Agree to her request just to be polite, but then continue your patrol after the woman is out of sight.
    D. Find a bystander who will agree to watch the shopping bag for her.

15. You are on duty at a public building. It is nearly 6:00 P.M., and most employees have left for the day. You see two well-dressed men carrying an office calculating machine out of the building.
You SHOULD
   A. stop them and ask for an explanation
   B. follow them to see where they are going
   C. order them to put down the machine and leave the building immediately
   D. take no action since they do not look like burglars

16. You are on duty patrolling a public building. You have just tripped on the stairs and turned your ankle. The ankle hurts and is starting to swell.
What is the BEST thing to do?
   A. Take a taxi to a hospital emergency room, and from there have a hospital employee call your supervisor to explain the situation.
   B. First try soaking your foot in cold water for half an hour, then go off duty if you really cannot walk at all.
   C. Report the situation to your supervisor, explaining that you need prompt medical attention for your ankle.
   D. Find a place where you can sit until you are due to go off duty, then have a doctor look at your ankle.

17. One of your duties as a special officer (security officer) on night patrol in a public building is to check the washrooms to see that the taps are turned off and that there are no plumbing leaks.
Of the following possible reasons for this inspection, which is probably the MOST important reason?
   A. If the floor gets wet, someone might slip and fall the next morning.
   B. A running water tap might be a sign that there is an intruder in the building.
   C. A washroom flood could leak through the ceilings and walls below and cause a lot of damage.
   D. Leaks must be reported quickly so that repairs can be scheduled as soon as possible.

18. You are on duty at a public building. A department supervisor tells you that someone has left a suspicious-looking package in the hallway on his floor. You investigate, and you hear ticking in the parcel. You think it could be a bomb.
The FIRST thing you should do is to
   A. rapidly question employees on this floor to get a description of the person who left the package
   B. write down the description of the package and the name of the department supervisor
   C. notify your security headquarters that there may be a bomb in the building and that all personnel should be evacuated
   D. pick up the package carefully and remove it from the building as quickly as you can

Questions 19-22.

DIRECTIONS: Answer Questions 19 through 22 on the basis of the Fact Situation and the Report of Arrest form below. Questions 19 through 22 ask how the report form should be filled in based on the information given in the Fact Situation.

FACT SITUATION

Jesse Stein is a special officer (security officer) who is assigned to a welfare center at 435 East Smythe Street, Brooklyn. He was on duty there Thursday morning, February 1. At 10:30 A.M., a client named Jo Ann Jones, 40 years old, arrived with her ten-year-old son, Peter. Another client, Mary Alice Wiell, 45 years old, immediately began to insult Mrs. Jones. When Mrs. Jones told her to "go away," Mrs. Wiell pulled out a long knife. The special officer (security officer) intervened and requested Mrs. Wiell to drop the knife. She would not, and he had to use necessary force to disarm her. He arrested her on charges of disorderly conduct, harassment, and possession of a dangerous weapon. Mrs. Wiell lives at 118 Heally Street, Brooklyn, Apartment 4F, and she is unemployed. The reason for her aggressive behavior is not known.

```
REPORT OF ARREST

(01)_____      (08)_____
    (Prisoner's surname) (first) (initial)    (Precinct)

(02)_____      (09)_____
    (Address)                                 (Date of arrest)
                                              (Month, Day)

(03)_____ (04)_____ (05)_____   (10)_____
    (Date of birth) (Age)    (Sex)            (Time of arrest)

(06)_____ (07)_____   (11)_____
    (Occupation)      (Where employed)        (Place of arrest)

(12)_____
    (Specific offenses)

(13)_____      (14)_____
    (Arresting Officer)                       (Officer's No.)
```

19. What entry should be made in Blank 01?   19.____
    A. Jo Ann Jones   B. Jones, Jo Ann
    C. Mary Wiell   D. Wiell, Mary A.

20. Which of the following should be entered in Blank 04?   20.____
    A. 40   B. 40's   C. 45   D. Middle-aged

21. Which of the following should be entered in Blank 09?
    A. Wednesday, February 1, 10:30 A.M.
    B. February 1
    C. Thursday morning, February 2
    D. Morning, February 4

    21._____

22. Of the following, which would be the BEST entry to make in Blank 11?
    A. Really Street Welfare Center
    B. Brooklyn
    C. 435 E. Smythe St., Brooklyn
    D. 118 Heally St., Apt. 4F

    22._____

Questions 23-27.

DIRECTIONS: Answer Questions 23 through 27 on the basis of the information given in the Report of Loss or Theft that appears below.

```
REPORT OF LOSS OR THEFT        Date: 12/4    Time: 9:15 a.m.
Complaint made by:  Richard Aldridge        [ ] Owner
                    306 S. Walter St.       [x] Other - explain:
                                            Head of Acctg. Dept.

Type of property: Typewriter                 Value: $150.00
Description: IBM electric model #110
Location: 768 N Margin Ave., Accounting Dept., 3rd Floor
Time: Overnight 12/3 - 12/4
Circumstances: Mr. Aldridge reports he arrived at work 8:45 A.M.,
found office door open and machine missing. Nothing else reported
missing. I investigated and found signs of forced entry: door lock
was broken.           Signature of Reporting Officer: B.L. Ramirez
Notify:
  [ ]  Building & Grounds Office, 768 N. Margin Ave.
  [ ]  Lost Property Office, 110 Brand Ave.
  [x]  Security Office, 703 N. Wide Street
```

23. The person who made this complaint is
    A. a secretary   B. a security officer
    C. Richard Aldridge   D. B.L. Ramirez

    23._____

24. The report concerns a typewriter that has been 24. ___
    A. lost   B. damaged   C. stolen   D. sold

25. The person who took the typewriter probably entered the 25. ___
    office through
    A. a door   B. a window   C. the roof   D. the basement

26. When did the head of the Accounting Department first 26. ___
    notice that the typewriter was missing?
    A. December 4 at 9:15 A.M.   B. December 4 at 8:45 A.M.
    C. The night of December 3   D. The night of December 4

27. The event described in the report took place at 27. ___
    A. 306 South Walter Street   B. 768 North Margin Avenue
    C. 110 Brand Avenue   D. 703 North Wide Street

Questions 28-33.

DIRECTIONS: Answer Questions 28 through 33 on the basis of the instructions, the code, and the sample question given below.

Assume that a special officer(security officer) at a certain location is equipped with a two-way radio to keep him in constant touch with his security headquarters. Radio messages and replies are given in code form, as follows:

Radio Code for Situation	J P M F B
Radio Code for Action to be Taken	o r a z q
Radio Response for Action Being Taken	1 2 3 4 5

Assume that each of the above capital letters is the radio code for a particular type of situation, that the small letter below each capital letter is the radio code for the action a special officer (security officer) is directed to take, and that the number directly below each small letter is the radio response a special officer (security officer) should make to indicate what action was actually taken.

In each of the following Questions 28 through 33, the code letter for the action directed (Column 2) and the code number for the action taken (Column 3) should correspond to the capital letters in Column 1.

If only Column 2 is different from Column 1, mark your answer A.

If only Column 3 is different from Column 1, mark your answer B.

If both Column 2 and Column 3 are different from Column 1, mark your answer C.

If both Columns 2 and 3 are the same as Column 1, mark your answer D.

SAMPLE QUESTION

Column 1	Column 2	Column 3
JPFMB	orzaq	12453

The code letters in Column 2 are correct, but the numbers 53 in Column 3 should be 35. Therefore, the answer is B.

	Column 1	Column 2	Column 3	
28.	PBFJM	rqzoa	25413	28.___
29.	MPFBJ	zrqao	32541	29.___
30.	JBFPM	oqzra	15432	30.___
31.	BJPMF	qaroz	51234	31.___
32.	PJFMB	rozaq	21435	32.___
33.	FJBMP	zoqra	41532	33.___

Questions 34-40.

DIRECTIONS: Questions 34 through 40 are based on the instructions given below. Study the instructions and the sample question; then answer Questions 34 through 40 on the basis of this information

INSTRUCTIONS:

In each of the following Questions 34 through 40, the 3-line name and address in Column 1 is the master-list entry, and the 3-line entry in Column 2 is the information to be checked against the master list.

If there is one line that does not match, mark your answer A.

If there are two lines that do not match, mark your answer B.

If all three lines do not match, mark your answer C.

If the lines all match exactly, mark your answer D.

SAMPLE QUESTION:

Column 1

Mark L. Field
11-09 Prince Park Blvd.
Bronx, N.Y. 11402

Column 2

Mark L. Field
11-99 Prince Park Way
Bronx, N.Y. 11401

The first lines in each column match exactly. The second lines do not match, since 11-09 does not match 11-99 and Blvd. does not match Way. The third lines do not match either, since 11402 does not match 1140<u>1</u>. Therefore, there are two lines that do not match and the correct answer is B.

	Column 1	Column 2	
34.	Jerome A. Jackson 1243 14th Avenue New York, N.Y. 10023	Jerome A. Johnson 1234 14th Avenue New York, N.Y. 10023	34.____
35.	Sophie Strachtheim 33-28 Connecticut Ave. Far Rockaway, N.Y. 11697	Sophie Strachtheim 33-28 Connecticut Ave. Far Rockaway, N.Y. 11697	35.____
36.	Elisabeth N.T. Gorrell 256 Exchange St. New York, N.Y. 10013	Elizabeth N.T. Gorrell 256 Exchange St. New York, N.Y. 10013	36.____
37.	Maria J. Gonzalez 7516 E. Sheepshead Rd. Brooklyn, N.Y. 11240	Maria J. Gonzalez 7516 N. Shepshead Rd. Brooklyn, N.Y. 11240	37.____
38.	Leslie B. Brautenweiler 21 57A Seiler Terr. Flushing, N.Y. 11367	Leslie B. Brautenwieler 21-75A Seiler Terr. Flushing, N.J. 11367	38.____
39.	Rigoberto J. Peredes 157 Twin Towers, #18F Tottenville, S.I., N.Y.	Rigoberto J. Peredes 157 Twin Towers, #18F Tottenville, S.I., N.Y.	39.____
40.	Pietro F. Albino P.O. Box 7548 Floral Park, N.Y. 11005	Pietro F. Albina P.O. Box 7458 Floral Park, N.Y. 11005	40.____

KEY (CORRECT ANSWERS)

1. D	11. A	21. B	31. A
2. C	12. D	22. C	32. D
3. B	13. C	23. C	33. A
4. D	14. B	24. C	34. B
5. B	15. A	25. A	35. D
6. A	16. C	26. B	36. A
7. C	17. C	27. B	37. A
8. D	18. C	28. D	38. C
9. D	19. D	29. C	39. D
10. D	20. C	30. B	40. B

EXAMINATION SECTION

TEST 1

DIRECTIONS: Each question or incomplete statement is followed by several suggested answers or completions. Select the one that BEST answers the question or completes the statement. *PRINT THE LETTER OF THE CORRECT ANSWER IN THE SPACE AT THE RIGHT.*

1. Of the following, the MOST important single factor in any building security program is
   A. a fool-proof employee identification system
   B. an effective control of entrances and exits
   C. bright illumination of all outside areas
   D. clearly marking public and non-public areas

2. There is general agreement that the BEST criterion of what is a good physical security system in a large public building is
   A. the number of uniformed officers needed to patrol sensitive areas
   B. how successfully the system prevents rather than detects violations
   C. the number of persons caught in the act of committing criminal offenses
   D. how successfully the system succeeds in maintaining good public relations

3. Which one of the following statements MOST correctly expresses the chief reason why women were made eligible for appointment to the position of officer?
   A. Certain tasks in security protection can be performed best by assigning women.
   B. More women than men are available to fill many vacancies in this position.
   C. The government wants more women in law enforcement because of their better attendance records.
   D. Women can no longer be barred from any government jobs because of sex.

4. The MOST BASIC purpose of patrol by officers is to
   A. eliminate as much as possible the opportunity for successful misconduct
   B. investigate criminal complaints and accident cases
   C. give prompt assistance to employees and citizens in distress or requesting their help
   D. take persons into custody who commit criminal offenses against persons and property

5. The highest quality of patrol service is MOST generally obtained by
   A. frequently changing the post assignments of each officer
   B. assigning officers to posts of equal size
   C. assigning problem officers to the least desirable posts
   D. assigning the same officers to the same posts

6. The one of the following requirements which is MOST essential to the successful performance of patrol duty by individual officers is their
   A. ability to communicate effectively with higher-level officers
   B. prompt signalling according to a prescribed schedule to insure post coverages at all times
   C. knowledge of post conditions and post hazards
   D. willingness to cover large areas during periods of critical manpower shortages

7. Officers on patrol are constantly warned to be on the alert for suspicious persons, actions, and circumstances.
   With this in mind, a senior officer should emphasize the need for them to
   A. be cautious and suspicious when dealing officially with any civilian regardless of the latter's overt actions or the circumstances surrounding his dealings with the police
   B. keep looking for the unusual persons, actions, and circumstances on their posts and pay less attention to the usual
   C. take aggressive police action immediately against any unusual person or condition detected on their posts, regardless of any other circumstances
   D. become thoroughly familiar with the usual on their posts so as to be better able to detect the unusual

8. Of primary importance in the safeguarding of property from theft is a good central lock and key issuance and control system.
   Which one of the following recommendations about maintaining such a control system would be LEAST acceptable?
   A. In selecting locks to be used for the various gates, building, and storage areas, consideration should be given to the amount of security desired.
   B. Master keys should have no markings that will identify them as such and the list of holders of these keys should be frequently reviewed to determine the continuing necessity for the individuals having them.
   C. Whenever keys for outside doors or gates or for other doors which permit access to important buildings and areas are misplaced, the locks should be immediately changed or replaced pending an investigation.
   D. Whenever an employee fails to return a borrowed key at the time specified, a prompt investigation should be made by the security force.

9. In a crowded building, a fire develops in the basement, and smoke enters the crowded rooms on the first floor.
   Of the following, the BEST action for an officer to take after an alarm is turned in is to
   A. call out a warning that the building is on fire and that everyone should evacuate because of the immediate danger
   B. call all of the officers together for an emergency meeting and discuss a plan of action

C. immediately call for assistance from the local police station to help in evacuating the crowd
D. tell everyone that there is a fire in the building next door and that they should move out onto the streets through available exits

10. Which of the following is in a key position to carry out successfully a safety program of an agency? The
    A. building engineer
    B. bureau chiefs
    C. immediate supervisors
    D. public relations director

11. It is GENERALLY considered that a daily roll call inspection, which checks to see that the officers and their equipment are in good order, is
    A. *desirable*, chiefly because it informs the superior officer what men will have to purchase new uniforms within a month
    B. *desirable*, chiefly because the public forms their impressions of the organization from the appearance of the officers
    C. *undesirable*, chiefly because this kind of daily inspection unnecessarily delays officers in getting to their assigned patrol posts
    D. *undesirable*, chiefly because roll call inspection usually misses individuals reporting to work late

12. A supervising officer in giving instructions to a group of officers on the principles of accident investigation remarked, "A conclusion that appears reasonable will often be changed by exploring a factor of apparently little importance".
    Which one of the following precautions does this statement emphasize as MOST important in any accident investigation?
    A. Every accident clue should be fully investigated.
    B. Accidents should not be too promptly investigated.
    C. Only specially trained officers should investigate accidents.
    D. Conclusions about accident causes are highly unreliable.

13. On a rainy day, a senior officer found that 9 of his 50 officers reported to work.
    What percentage of his officers was ABSENT?
    A. 18%   B. 80%   C. 82%   D. 90%

14. Officer A and Officer B work at the same post on the same days, but their hours are different. Officer A comes to work at 9:00 A.M. and leaves at 5:00 P.M., with a lunch period between 12:15 P.M. and 1:15 P.M. Officer B comes to work at 10:50 A.M. and works until 6:50 P.M., and he takes an hour for lunch between 3:00 P.M. and 4:00 P.M. What is the total amount of time between 9:00 A.M. and 6:50 P.M. that only ONE officer will be on duty?
    A. 4 hours
    B. 4 hours and 40 minutes
    C. 5 hours
    D. 5 hours and 40 minutes

15. An officer's log recorded the following attendance of 30 officers:

Monday	20 present;	10 absent
Tuesday	28 present;	2 absent
Wednesday	30 present;	0 absent
Thursday	21 present;	9 absent
Friday	16 present;	14 absent
Saturday	11 present;	19 absent
Sunday	14 present;	16 absent

On the average, how many men were present on the weekdays (Monday - Friday)?
A. 21   B. 23   C. 25   D. 27

16. An angry woman is being questioned by an officer when she begins shouting abuses at him.
The BEST of the following procedures for the officer to follow is to
A. leave the room until she has cooled off
B. politely ignore anything she says
C. place her under arrest by handcuffing her to a fixed object
D. warn her that he will have to use force to restrain her making remarks

17. Of the following, which is NOT a recommended practice for an officer placing a woman offender under arrest?
A. Assume that the offender is an innocent and virtuous person and treat her accordingly.
B. Protect himself from attack by the woman.
C. Refrain from using excessive physical force on the offender.
D. Make the public aware that he is not abusing the woman.

Questions 18-21.

DIRECTIONS: Questions 18 through 21 are to be answered SOLELY on the basis of the following passage.

Specific measures for prevention of pilferage will be based on careful analysis of the conditions at each agency. The most practical and effective method to control casual pilferage is the establishment of psychological deterrents.

One of the most common means of discouraging casual pilferage is to search individuals leaving the agency at unannounced times and places. These spot searches may occasionally detect attempts at theft but greater value is realized by bringing to the attention of individuals the fact that they may be apprehended if they do attempt the illegal removal of property.

An aggressive security education program is an effective means of convincing employees that they have much more to lose than they do to gain by engaging in acts of theft. It is important for all employees to realize that pilferage is morally wrong no matter how insignificant the value of the item which is taken. In establishing any deterrent to casual pilferage, security officers must not lose sight of the fact that most employees are honest and disapprove of thievery. Mutual respect between security personnel and other employees of the agency must be maintained if the facility is to be protected from other more dangerous forms of human hazards. Any security measure which infringes on the human rights or dignity of others will jeopardize, rather than enhance, the overall protection of the agency.

18. The $100,000 yearly inventory of an agency revealed that $50 worth of goods had been stolen; the only individuals with access to the stolen materials were the employees. Of the following measures, which would the author of the preceding paragraph MOST likely recommend to a security officer?
    A. Conduct an intensive investigation of all employees to find the culprit.
    B. Make a record of the theft, but take no investigative or disciplinary action against any employee.
    C. Place a tight security check on all future movements of personnel.
    D. Remove the remainder of the material to an area with much greater security.

19. What does the passage imply is the percentage of employees whom a security officer should expect to be honest?
    A. No employee can be expected to be honest all of the time
    B. Just 50%
    C. Less than 50%
    D. More than 50%

20. According to the passage, the security officer would use which of the following methods to minimize theft in buildings with many exits when his staff is very small?
    A. Conduct an inventory of all material and place a guard near that which is most likely to be pilfered.
    B. Inform employees of the consequences of legal prosecution for pilfering.
    C. Close off the unimportant exits and have all his men concentrate on a few exits.
    D. Place a guard at each exit and conduct a casual search of individuals leaving the premises.

21. Of the following, the title BEST suited for this passage is:
    A. Control Measures for Casual Pilfering
    B. Detecting the Potential Pilferer
    C. Financial Losses Resulting from Pilfering
    D. The Use of Moral Persuasion in Physical Security

22. Of the following first aid procedures, which will cause the GREATEST harm in treating a fracture?
    A. Control hemorrhages by applying direct pressure
    B. Keep the broken portion from moving about
    C. Reset a protruding bone by pressing it back into place
    D. Treat the suffering person for shock

23. During a snowstorm, a man comes to you complaining of frostbitten hands.
PROPER first aid treatment in this case is to
A. place the hands under hot running water
B. place the hands in lukewarm water
C. call a hospital and wait for medical aid
D. rub the hands in melting snow

24. While on duty, an officer sees a woman apparently in a state of shock.
Of the following, which one is NOT a symptom of shock?
A. Eyes lacking luster
B. A cold, moist forehead
C. A shallow, irregular breathing
D. A strong, throbbing pulse

25. You notice a man entering your building who begins coughing violently, has shortness of breath, and complains of severe chest pains.
These symptoms are GENERALLY indicative of
A. a heart attack   B. a stroke
C. internal bleeding D. an epileptic seizure

26. When an officer is required to record the rolled fingerprint impressions of a prisoner on the standard fingerprint form, the technique recommended by the F.B.I. as MOST likely to result in obtaining clear impressions is to roll
A. all fingers away from the center of the prisoner's body
B. all fingers toward the center of the prisoner's body
C. the thumbs away from and the other fingers toward the center of the prisoner's body
D. the thumbs toward and the other fingers away from the center of the prisoner's body

27. The principle which underlies the operation and use of a lie detector machine is that
A. a person who is not telling the truth will be able to give a consistent story
B. a guilty mind will unconsciously associate ideas in a very indicative manner
C. the presence of emotional stress in a person will result in certain abnormal physical reactions
D. many individuals are not afraid to lie

Questions 28-32.

DIRECTIONS: Questions 28 through 32 are based SOLELY on the following diagram and the paragraph preceding this group of questions. The paragraph will be divided into two statements. Statement one (1) consists of information given to the senior officer by an agency director; *this information will detail the specific security objectives the senior officer has to meet.* Statement two (2) gives the resources available to the senior officer.

NOTE: The questions are correctly answered only when all of the agency's objectives have been met and when the officer has used all his resources efficiently (i.e., to their maximum effectiveness) in meeting these objectives. All X's in the diagram indicate possible locations of officers' posts. Each X has a corresponding number which is to be used when referring to that location.

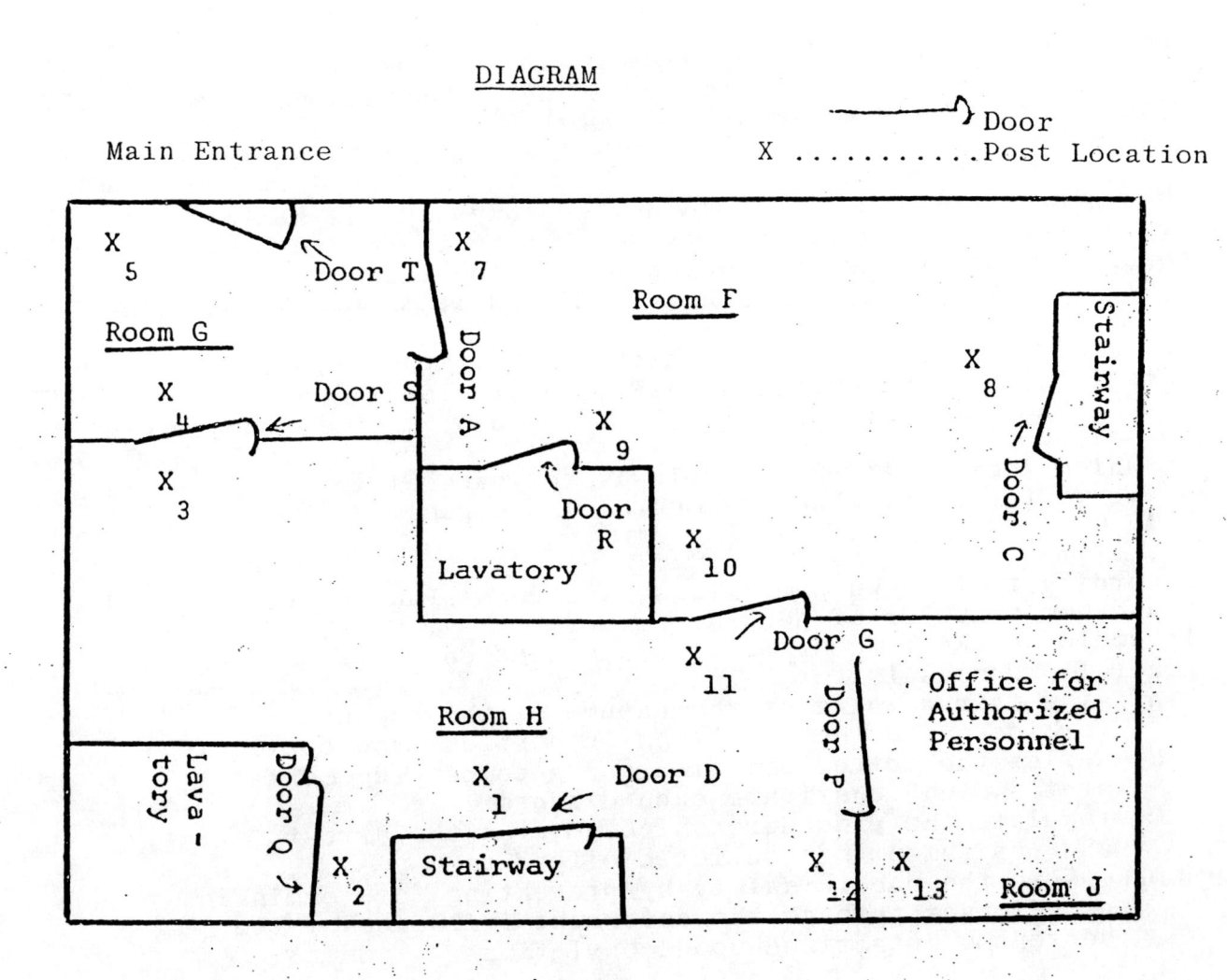

DIAGRAM

Main Entrance

→) Door
X .... Post Location

- Room G (contains X5, X4, X3; Door T, Door S)
- Room F (contains X7, X9, X8; Door A, Door R, Door C to Stairway)
- Lavatory (Door R)
- Room H (contains X1, X10, X11; Door D, Stairway, Door Q to Lavatory, X2)
- Office for Authorized Personnel (Door G, Door P)
- Room J (contains X12, X13)

PARAGRAPH

STATEMENT 1: Room G will be the public intake room from which persons will be directed to Room F or Room H; under no circumstances are they to enter the wrong room, and they are not to move from Room F to Room H or vice-versa. A minimum of two officers must be in each room frequented by the public at all times, and they are to keep unauthorized individuals from going to the second floor or into restricted areas. All usable entrances or exits must be covered.

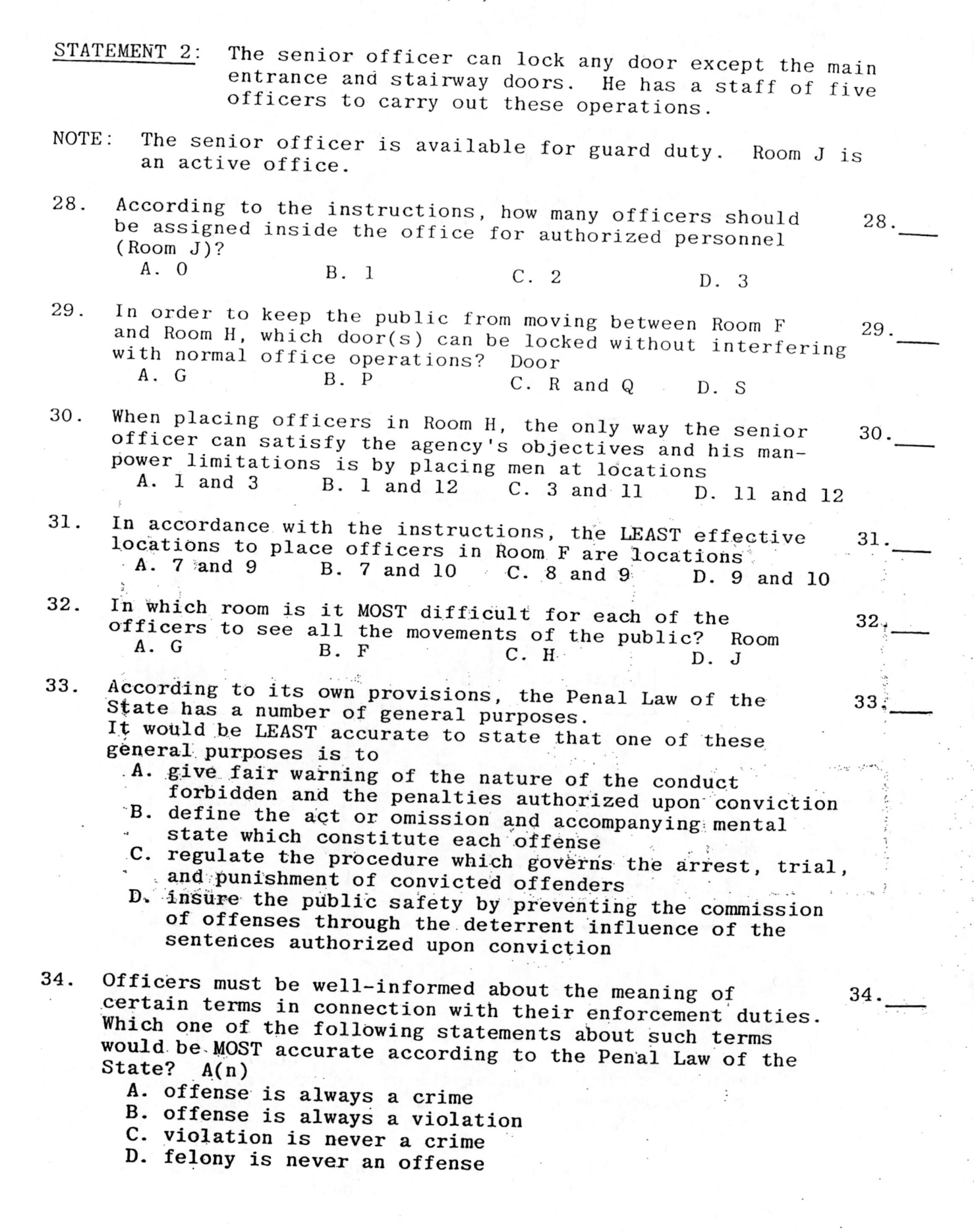

STATEMENT 2: The senior officer can lock any door except the main entrance and stairway doors. He has a staff of five officers to carry out these operations.

NOTE: The senior officer is available for guard duty. Room J is an active office.

28. According to the instructions, how many officers should be assigned inside the office for authorized personnel (Room J)?
    A. 0   B. 1   C. 2   D. 3

29. In order to keep the public from moving between Room F and Room H, which door(s) can be locked without interfering with normal office operations? Door
    A. G   B. P   C. R and Q   D. S

30. When placing officers in Room H, the only way the senior officer can satisfy the agency's objectives and his manpower limitations is by placing men at locations
    A. 1 and 3   B. 1 and 12   C. 3 and 11   D. 11 and 12

31. In accordance with the instructions, the LEAST effective locations to place officers in Room F are locations
    A. 7 and 9   B. 7 and 10   C. 8 and 9   D. 9 and 10

32. In which room is it MOST difficult for each of the officers to see all the movements of the public? Room
    A. G   B. F   C. H   D. J

33. According to its own provisions, the Penal Law of the State has a number of general purposes.
    It would be LEAST accurate to state that one of these general purposes is to
    A. give fair warning of the nature of the conduct forbidden and the penalties authorized upon conviction
    B. define the act or omission and accompanying mental state which constitute each offense
    C. regulate the procedure which governs the arrest, trial, and punishment of convicted offenders
    D. insure the public safety by preventing the commission of offenses through the deterrent influence of the sentences authorized upon conviction

34. Officers must be well-informed about the meaning of certain terms in connection with their enforcement duties. Which one of the following statements about such terms would be MOST accurate according to the Penal Law of the State? A(n)
    A. offense is always a crime
    B. offense is always a violation
    C. violation is never a crime
    D. felony is never an offense

35. According to the Penal Law of the State, the one of the following elements which must ALWAYS be present in order to justify the arrest of a person for criminal assault is
    A. the infliction of an actual physical injury
    B. an intent to cause an injury
    C. a threat to inflict a physical injury
    D. the use of some kind of weapon

36. A recent law of the State defines who are police officers and who are peace officers.
    The official title of this law is: The
    A. Criminal Code of Procedure
    B. Law of Criminal Procedure
    C. Criminal Procedure Law
    D. Code of Criminal Procedure

37. If you are required to appear in court to testify as the complainant in a criminal action, it would be MOST important for you to
    A. confine your answers to the questions asked when you are testifying
    B. help the prosecutor even if some exaggeration in your testimony may be necessary
    C. be as fair as possible to the defendant even if some details have to be omitted from your testimony
    D. avoid contradicting other witnesses testifying against the defendant

38. A senior officer is asked by the television news media to explain to the public what happened on his post during an important incident.
    When speaking with departmental permission in front of the tape recorders and cameras, the senior officer can give the MOST favorable impression of himself and his department by
    A. refusing to answer any questions but remaining calm in front of the cameras
    B. giving a detailed report of the wrong decisions made by his agency for handling the particular incident
    C. presenting the appropriate factual information in a competent way
    D. telling what should have been done during the incident and how such incidents will be handled in the future

39. Of the following suggested guidelines for officers, the one which is LEAST likely to be effective in promoting good manners and courtesy in their daily contacts with the public is:
    A. Treat inquiries by telephone in the same manner as those made in person
    B. Never look into the face of the person to whom you are speaking
    C. Never give misinformation in answer to any inquiry on a matter on which you are uncertain of the facts
    D. Show respect and consideration in both trivial and important contacts with the public

40. Assume you are an officer who has had a record of submitting late weekly reports and that you are given an order by your supervisor which is addressed to all line officers. The order states that weekly reports will be replaced by twice-weekly reports.
The MOST logical conclusion for you to make, of the following, is:
   A. Fully detailed information was missing from your past reports
   B. Most officers have submitted late reports
   C. The supervisor needs more timely information
   D. The supervisor is attempting to punish you for your past late reports

41. A young man with long hair and "mod" clothing makes a complaint to an officer about the rudeness of another officer.
If the senior officer is not on the premises, the officer receiving the complaint should
   A. consult with the officer who is being accused to see if the youth's story is true
   B. refer the young man to central headquarters
   C. record the complaint made against his fellow officer and ask the youth to wait until he can locate the senior officer
   D. search for the senior officer and bring him back to the site of the complainant

42. During a demonstration, which area should ALWAYS be kept clear of demonstrators?
   A. Water fountains   B. Seating areas
   C. Doorways   D. Restrooms

43. During demonstrations, an officer's MOST important duty is to
   A. aid the agency's employees to perform their duties
   B. promptly arrest those who might cause incidents
   C. promptly disperse the crowds of demonstrators
   D. keep the demonstrators from disrupting order

44. Of the following, what is the FIRST action a senior officer should take if a demonstration develops in his area without advance warning?
   A. Call for additional assistance from the police department
   B. Find the leaders of the demonstrators and discuss their demands
   C. See if the demonstrators intend to break the law
   D. Inform his superiors of the event taking place

45. If a senior officer is informed in the morning that a demonstration will take place during the afternoon at his assigned location, he should assemble his officers to discuss the nature and aspects of this demonstration.
Of the following, the subject which it is LEAST important to discuss during this meeting is

A. making a good impression if an officer is called before the television cameras for a personal interview
B. the known facts and causes of the demonstration
C. the attitude and expected behavior of the demonstrators
D. the individual responsibilities of the officers during the demonstration

46. A male officer has probable reason to believe that a group of women occupying the ladies' toilet are using illicit drugs.
The BEST action, of the following, for the officer to take is to
    A. call for assistance and, with the aid of such assistance, enter the toilet and escort the occupants outside
    B. ignore the situation but recommend that the ladies' toilet be closed temporarily
    C. immediately rush into the ladies' toilet and search the occupants therein
    D. knock on the door of the ladies' toilet and ask their permission to enter so that he will not be accused of trying to molest them

47. Assume that you know that a group of demonstrators will not cooperate with your request to throw handbills in a waste basket instead of on the sidewalk. You ask one of the leaders of the group, who agrees with you, to speak to the demonstrators and ask for their cooperation in this matter.
Your request of the group leader is
    A. *desirable*, chiefly because an officer needs civilians to control the public since the officer is usually unfriendly to the views of public groups
    B. *undesirable*, chiefly because an officer should never request a civilian to perform his duties
    C. *desirable*, chiefly because the appeal of an acknowledged leader helps in gaining group cooperation
    D. *undesirable*, chiefly because an institutional leader is motivated to maneuver a situation to gain his own personal advantage

48. A vague letter received from a female employee in the agency accuses an officer of improper conduct.
The initial investigative interview by the senior officer assigned to check the accusation should GENERALLY be with the
    A. accused officer
    B. female employee
    C. highest superior about disciplinary action against the officer
    D. immediate supervisor of the female employee

Questions 49-50.

DIRECTIONS: Questions 49 and 50 are to be answered SOLELY on the basis of the information in the following paragraph.

The personal conduct of each member of the Department is the primary factor in promoting desirable police-community relations. Tact, patience, and courtesy shall be strictly observed under all circumstances. A favorable public attitude toward the police must be earned; it is influenced by the personal conduct and attitude of each member of the force, by his personal integrity and courteous manner, by his respect for due process of law, by his devotion to the principles of justice, fairness, and <u>impartiality</u>.

49. According to the preceding paragraph, what is the BEST action an officer can take in dealing with people in a neighborhood?
    A. Assist neighborhood residents by doing favors for them.
    B. Give special attention to the community leaders in order to be able to control them effectively.
    C. Behave in an appropriate manner and give all community members the same just treatment.
    D. Prepare a plan detailing what he, the officer, wants to do for the community and submit it for approval.

50. As used in the paragraph, the word <u>impartiality</u> means most nearly
    A. observant
    B. unbiased
    C. righteousness
    D. honesty

KEY (CORRECT ANSWERS)

1. B	11. B	21. A	31. D	41. C
2. B	12. A	22. C	32. C	42. C
3. A	13. C	23. B	33. C	43. D
4. A	14. D	24. D	34. C	44. D
5. D	15. B	25. A	35. A	45. A
6. C	16. B	26. D	36. C	46. A
7. D	17. A	27. C	37. A	47. C
8. C	18. B	28. A	38. C	48. B
9. D	19. D	29. A	39. B	49. C
10. C	20. B	30. B	40. C	50. B

TEST 2

DIRECTIONS: Each question or incomplete statement is followed by several suggested answers or completions. Select the one that BEST answers the question or completes the statement. *PRINT THE LETTER OF THE CORRECT ANSWER IN THE SPACE AT THE RIGHT.*

Questions 1-5.

DIRECTIONS: Questions 1 through 5 consist of short paragraphs. Each paragraph contains one word which is INCORRECTLY used because it is NOT in keeping with the meaning of the paragraph. Find the word in each paragraph which is INCORRECTLY used, and then select as the answer the suggested word which should be substituted for the incorrectly used word.

SAMPLE QUESTION

In determining who is to do the work in your unit, you will have to decide just who does what from day to day. One of your lowest responsibilities is to assign work so that everybody gets a fair share and that everyone can do his part well.
   A. new   B. old   C. important   D. performance

EXPLANATION

The word which is NOT in keeping with the meaning of the paragraph is "lowest". This is the INCORRECTLY used word. The suggested word "important" would be in keeping with the meaning of the paragraph and should be substituted for "lowest". Therefore, the CORRECT answer is Choice C.

1. If really good practice in the elimination of preventable injuries is to be achieved and held in any establishment, top management must refuse full and definite responsibility and must apply a good share of its attention to the task.
   A. accept   B. avoidable   C. duties   D. problem

1.___

2. Recording the human face for identification is by no means the only service performed by the camera in the field of investigation. When the trial of any issue takes place, a word picture is sought to be distorted to the court of incidents, occurrences, or events which are in dispute.
   A. appeals   B. description
   C. portrayed   D. deranged

2.___

3. In the collection of physical evidence, it cannot be emphasized too strongly that a haphazard systematic search at the scene of the crime is vital. Nothing must be overlooked. Often the only leads in a case will come from the results of this search.

3.___

A. important B. investigation
C. proof   D. thorough

4. If an investigator has reason to suspect that the witness is mentally stable or a habitual drunkard, he should leave no stone unturned in his investigation to determine if the witness was under the influence of liquor or drugs, or was mentally unbalanced either at the time of the occurrence to which he testified or at the time of the trial.
   A. accused   B. clue   C. deranged   D. question

4._____

5. The use of records is a valuable step in crime investigation and is the main reason every department should maintain accurate reports. Crimes are not committed through the use of departmental records alone but from the use of all records, of almost every type, wherever they may be found and whenever they give any incidental information regarding the criminal.
   A. accidental   B. necessary   C. reported   D. solved

5._____

Questions 6-8.

DIRECTIONS: Questions 6 through 8 are to be answered SOLELY on the basis of the following passage.

The mass media are an integral part of the daily life of virtually every American. Among these media, the youngest, television, is the most persuasive. Ninety-five percent of American homes have at least one television set, and on the average that set is in use for about 40 hours each week. The central place of television in American life makes this medium the focal point of a growing national concern over the effects of media portrayals of violence on the values, attitudes, and behavior of an ever increasing audience.

In our concern about violence and its causes, it is easy to make television a scapegoat. But we emphasize the fact that there is no simple answer to the problem of violence -- no single explanation of its causes, and no single prescription for its control. It should be remembered that America also experienced high levels of crime and violence in periods before the advent of television.

The problem of balance, taste, and artistic merit in entertaining programs on television are complex. We cannot countenance government censorship of television. Nor would we seek to impose arbitrary limitations on programming which might jeopardize television's ability to deal in dramatic presentations with controversial social issues. Nonetheless, we are deeply troubled by television's constant portrayal of violence, not in any genuine attempt to focus artistic expression on the human condition, but rather in pandering to a public preoccupation with violence that television itself has helped to generate.

6. According to the passage, television uses violence MAINLY
   A. to highlight the reality of everyday existence
   B. to satisfy the audience's hunger for destructive action
   C. to shape the values and attitudes of the public
   D. when it films documentaries concerning human conflict

6._____

7. Which one of the following statements is BEST supported by this passage?
   A. Early American history reveals a crime pattern which is not related to television.
   B. Programs should give presentations of social issues and never portray violent acts.
   C. Television has proven that entertainment programs can easily make the balance between taste and artistic merit a simple matter.
   D. Values and behavior should be regulated by governmental censorship.

8. Of the following, which word has the same meaning as *countenance*, as it is used in the above passage?
   A. approve   B. exhibit   C. oppose   D. reject

Questions 9-12.

DIRECTIONS: Questions 9 through 12 are to be answered SOLELY on the basis of the following graph relating to the burglary rate in the city, 1973 to 1978, inclusive.

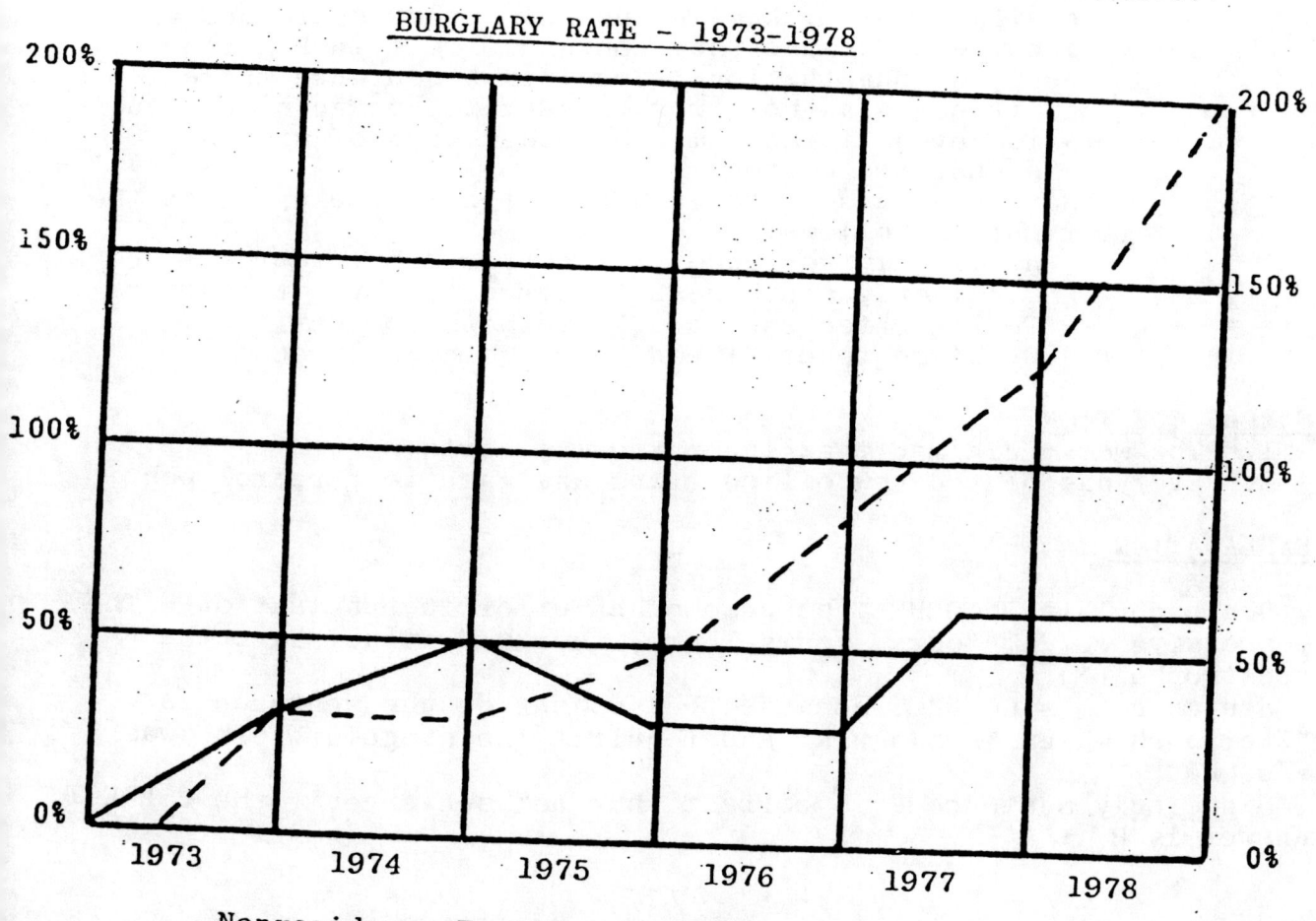

BURGLARY RATE - 1973-1978

———— Nonresidence Burglary Nighttime

- - - - - - Nonresidence Burglary Daytime

1973-1978

9. At the beginning of what year was the percentage increase in daytime and nighttime burglaries the SAME?
   A. 1974   B. 1975   C. 1976   D. 1978

10. In what year did the percentage of nighttime burglaries DECREASE?
    A. 1973   B. 1975   C. 1976   D. 1978

11. In what year was there the MOST rapid increase in the percentage of daytime non-residence burglaries?
    A. 1974   B. 1976   C. 1977   D. 1978

12. At the end of 1977, the actual number of nighttime burglaries committed
    A. was about 20%
    B. was 40%
    C. was 400
    D. cannot be determined from the information given

Questions 13-17.

DIRECTIONS: Questions 13 through 17 consist of two sentences numbered 1 and 2 taken from police officers' reports. Some of these sentences are correct according to ordinary formal English usage. Other sentences are incorrect because they contain errors in English usage or punctuation. Consider a sentence correct if it contains no errors in English usage or punctuation even if there may be other ways of writing the sentence correctly.
Mark your answer to each question in the space at the right as follows:
   A. If only sentence 1 is correct, but not sentence 2
   B. If only sentence 2 is correct, but not sentence 1
   C. If sentences 1 and 2 are both correct
   D. If sentences 1 and 2 are both incorrect

SAMPLE QUESTION
1. The woman claimed that the purse was her's.
2. Everyone of the new officers was assigned to a patrol post.

EXPLANATION

Sentence 1 is INCORRECT because of an error in punctuation. The possessive words, "ours, yours, hers, theirs," do not have the apostrophe (').
Sentence 2 is CORRECT because the subject of the sentence is "Everyone" which is singular and requires the singular verb "was assigned".
Since only sentence 2 is correct, but not sentence 1, the CORRECT answer is B.

13. 1. Either the patrolman or his sergeant are always ready to help the public.
    2. The sergeant asked the patrolman when he would finish the report.

5 (#2)

14. 1. The injured man could not hardly talk.
    2. Every officer had ought to hand in their reports on time.   14.____

15. 1. Approaching the victim of the assault, two large bruises were noticed by me.   15.____
    2. The prisoner was arrested for assault, resisting arrest, and use of a deadly weapon.

16. 1. A copy of the orders, which had been prepared by the captain, was given to each patrolman.   16.____
    2. It's always necessary to inform an arrested person of his constitutional rights before asking him any questions.

17. 1. To prevent further bleeding, I applied a tourniquet to the wound.   17.____
    2. John Rano a senior officer was on duty at the time of the accident.

Questions 18-25.

DIRECTIONS: Answer each of Questions 18 through 25 SOLELY on the basis of the statement preceding the questions.

18. The criminal is one whose habits have been erroneously developed or, we should say, developed in anti-social patterns, and therefore the task of dealing with him is not one of punishment, but of treatment.   18.____
    The basic principle expressed in this statement is BEST illustrated by the
    A. emphasis upon rehabilitation in penal institutions
    B. prevalence of capital punishment for murder
    C. practice of imposing heavy fines for minor violations
    D. legal provision for trial by jury in criminal cases

19. The writ of habeas corpus is one of the great guarantees of personal liberty.   19.____
    Of the following, the BEST justification for this statement is that the writ of habeas corpus is frequently used to
    A. compel the appearance in court of witnesses who are outside the state
    B. obtain the production of books and records at a criminal trial
    C. secure the release of a person improperly held in custody
    D. prevent the use of deception in obtaining testimony of reluctant witnesses

20. Fifteen persons suffered effects of carbon dioxide asphyxiation shortly before noon recently in a seventh-floor pressing shop. The accident occurred in a closed room where six steam presses were in operation. Four men and one woman were overcome.   20.____
    Of the following, the MOST probable reason for the fact that so many people were affected simultaneously is that
    A. women evidently show more resistance to the effects of carbon dioxide than men
    B. carbon dioxide is an odorless and colorless gas

C. carbon dioxide is lighter than air
D. carbon dioxide works more quickly at higher altitudes

21. Lay the patient on his stomach, one arm extended directly overhead, the other arm bent at the elbow, and with the face turned outward and resting on hand or forearm.
To the officer who is skilled at administering first aid, these instructions should IMMEDIATELY suggest
    A. application of artificial respiration
    B. treatment for third degree burns of the arm
    C. setting a dislocated shoulder
    D. control of capillary bleeding in the stomach

22. The soda and acid fire extinguisher is the hand extinguisher most commonly used by officers. The main body of the cylinder is filled with a mixture of water and bicarbonate of soda. In a separate interior compartment, at the top, is a small bottle of sulphuric acid. When the extinguisher is inverted, the acid spills into the solution below and starts a chemical reaction. The carbon dioxide thereby generated forces the solution from the extinguisher.
The officer who understands the operation of this fire extinguisher should know that it is LEAST likely to operate properly
    A. in basements or cellars
    B. in extremely cold weather
    C. when the reaction is of a chemical nature
    D. when the bicarbonate of soda is in solution

23. Suppose that, at a training lecture, you are told that many of the men in our penal institutions today are second and third offenders.
Of the following, the MOST valid inference you can make SOLELY on the basis of this statement is that
    A. second offenders are not easily apprehended
    B. patterns of human behavior are not easily changed
    C. modern laws are not sufficiently flexible
    D. laws do not breed crimes

24. In all societies of our level of culture, acts are committed which arouse censure severe enough to take the form of punishment by the government. Such acts are crimes, not because of their inherent nature, but because of their ability to arouse resentment and to stimulate repressive measures.
Of the following, the MOST valid inference which can be drawn from this statement is that
    A. society unjustly punishes acts which are inherently criminal
    B. many acts are not crimes but are punished by society because such acts threaten the lives of innocent people
    C. only modern society has a level of culture
    D. societies sometimes disagree as to what acts are crimes

25. Crime cannot be measured directly. Its amount must be inferred from the frequency of some occurrence connected with it; for example, crimes brought to the attention of the police, persons arrested, prosecutions, convictions, and other dispositions, such as probation or commitment. Each of these may be used as an index of the amount of crime. SOLELY on the basis of the foregoing statement, it is MOST correct to state that
    A. the incidence of crime cannot be estimated with any accuracy
    B. the number of commitments is usually greater than the number of probationary sentences
    C. the amount of crime is ordinarily directly correlated with the number of persons arrested
    D. a joint consideration of crimes brought to the attention of the police and the number of prosecutions undertaken gives little indication of the amount of crime in a locality

25._____

KEY (CORRECT ANSWERS)

1. B
2. A
3. D
4. C
5. D

6. B
7. A
8. A
9. A
10. B

11. D
12. D
13. D
14. D
15. B

16. C
17. A
18. A
19. C
20. B

21. A
22. B
23. B
24. D
25. C

EXAMINATION SECTION

TEST 1

DIRECTIONS: Each question or incomplete statement is followed by several suggested answers or completions. Select the one that BEST answers the question or completes the statement. *PRINT THE LETTER OF THE CORRECT ANSWER IN THE SPACE AT THE RIGHT.*

Questions 1-9.

DIRECTIONS: Questions 1 through 9 are to be answered SOLELY on the basis of the following information and the DIRECTORY OF SERVICES.

Officer Johnson has just been assigned to the North End Service Facility and is now on his post in the main lobby. The facility is open to the public from 9 A.M. to 5 P.M. each Monday through Friday, except on Thursdays when it is open from 9 A.M. to 7 P.M. The facility is closed on holidays.

Officer Johnson must ensure an orderly flow of visitors through the lobby of the facility. To accomplish this, Officer Johnson gives directions and provides routine information to clients and other members of the public who enter and leave the facility through the lobby.

In order to give directions and provide routine information to visitors, such as information concerning the location of services, Officer Johnson consults the Directory of Services shown below. Officer Johnson must ensure that clients are directed to the correct room for service and are sent to that room only during the hours that the particular service is available. When clients ask for the location of more than one service, they should be directed to go first to the service that will close soonest.

NORTH END SERVICE FACILITY

DIRECTORY OF SERVICES

Room	Type of Service	Days Available	Hours Open
101	Facility Receptionist	Monday, Tuesday, Wednesday, Friday Thursday	9 AM-5 PM 9 AM-7 PM
103	Photo Identification Cards	Monday, Wednesday, Friday	9 AM-12 Noon
104	Lost and Stolen Identification Cards	Wednesday, Thursday	9 AM-5 PM
105	Applications for Welfare/Food Stamps	Wednesday, Friday	1 PM-5 PM

DIRECTORY OF SERVICES
(CONT'D)

Room	Type of Service	Days Available	Hours Open
107	Recertification for Welfare/Food Stamps	Monday, Thursday	10 AM-12 Noon
108	Medicaid Applications	Tuesday, Wednesday	2 PM-5 PM
109	Medicaid Complaints	Tuesday, Wednesday	10 AM-2 PM
110, 111	Social Worker	Monday, Wednesday Tuesday, Friday Thursday	9 AM-12 Noon 1 PM-5 PM 9 AM-5 PM
114	Hearing Room (By appointment only)	Monday, Thursday	9 AM-5 PM
115	Hearing Information	Monday, Tuesday, Wednesday, Thursday, Friday	9 AM-1 PM
206, 207	Nutrition Aid	Monday, Wednesday, Friday Tuesday, Thursday	10 AM-2 PM 9 AM-12 Noon
215	Health Clinic	Monday, Tuesday, Wednesday, Friday Thursday	9 AM-5 PM 9 AM-7 PM
220	Facility Administrative Office	Monday, Tuesday, Wednesday, Thursday, Friday	9 AM-5 PM

1. It is Tuesday morning and Ms. Loretta Rogers, a client of the North End Service Facility, asks Officer Johnson where she should go in order to apply for Medicaid. Officer Johnson tells Ms. Rogers to go to Room ____ at ____.
   A. 108; 1:00 P.M.
   B. 109; 11:00 A.M.
   C. 108; 2:00 P.M.
   D. 109; 2:00 P.M.

2. On Friday at 11:00 A.M., Mrs. Ruth Ramos, a new client at the North End Service Facility, tells Officer Johnson that she wants to obtain a photo identification card and see a social worker.
   Officer Johnson should direct Mrs. Ramos to first go to Room
   A. 103   B. 104   C. 110   D. 220

3. On Friday at 10:30 A.M., a client at the North End Service Facility who is directed by Officer Johnson to go to Room 206 will be able to receive service regarding
   A. Recertification for Welfare/Food Stamps
   B. Hearing Information
   C. Medicaid Applications
   D. Nutrition Aid

4. At 9:00 A.M. on Monday, a client at the North End Service Facility who is directed by Officer Johnson to Room 101 for service will find
   A. Nutrition Aid   B. Facility Receptionist
   C. Health Clinic   D. Hearing Information

5. On Tuesday at 12:30 P.M., Mr. Paul Brown tells Officer Johnson that he lost his identification card and wants to obtain a new one as soon as possible.
   Officer Johnson should direct Mr. Brown to go to Room 104
   A. immediately
   B. at 1:00 P.M. that day
   C. at 9:00 A.M. on Wednesday
   D. at 2:00 P.M. on Friday

6. A client at the North End Service Facility explains to Officer Johnson that he wants to make an appointment with a Social Worker.
   The client should be directed to go to Room
   A. 104   B. 110   C. 115   D. 215

7. Ms. Alice Lee is a client at the North End Service Facility who has a 10:00 A.M. appointment on Thursday in the Hearing Room and does not know where to go.
   Officer Johnson should direct Ms. Lee to go to Room
   A. 101   B. 110   C. 112   D. 114

8. Officer Johnson is asked by a visitor which services are available on Thursdays between 5:00 P.M. and 7:00 P.M.
   Officer Johnson should inform the visitor that an available service during that time is
   A. Health Clinic   B. Medicaid Complaints
   C. Nutrition Aid   D. Social Worker

9. Mr. Jack Klein, a visitor to the North End Service Facility, asks Officer Johnson when and where he can file a complaint concerning Medicaid.
   Officer Johnson should inform Mr. Klein that he may go to Room
   A. 108 on Tuesday or Wednesday between 2:00 P.M. and 5:00 P.M.
   B. 109 on Tuesday or Wednesday between 10:00 A.M. and 2:00 P.M.
   C. 115 on Monday or Tuesday between 10:00 A.M. and 12:00 Noon
   D. 215 on Thursday between 9:00 A.M. and 7:00 P.M.

Questions 10-12.

DIRECTIONS: Questions 10 through 12 are to be answered SOLELY on the basis of the following information.

Security Officers should act in accordance with guidelines included in a manual provided to security staff. Assume that the following guidelines apply to Officers when in contact with visitors or clients in a facility:

1. Try to see things from the visitor's or client's point of view.
2. Ignore insulting comments.
3. Maintain a calm and patient manner.
4. Speak quietly, courteously, and tactfully.

10. Officer Renee Williams is patrolling the lobby area of her facility when she hears a client angrily yelling at the receptionist. She goes to investigate the situation and finds out from the receptionist that the client is one hour late for his appointment with a social worker who now has other appointments. The client demands to be seen by the social worker immediately. Officer Williams angrily tells the client that it is his own fault that he missed his appointment and he should stop bothering the receptionist and go home.
In this situation, Officer Williams' behavior towards the client is
    A. *proper*, chiefly because it is the client's fault that he missed his appointment
    B. *improper*, chiefly because security officers should stay calm and speak courteously when dealing with clients
    C. *proper*, chiefly because the client had yelled at the receptionist
    D. *improper*, chiefly because the security officer should have ignored the whole incident

11. During his tour, Officer Montgomery is passing through his facility's waiting room on the way to the cafeteria for a break. As Officer Montgomery passes by a visitor, the visitor mutters an insulting remark about the Officer's appearance. Officer Montgomery ignores the visitor and the remark and proceeds on his way to the cafeteria.
Officer Montgomery's action in this situation is
    A. *correct*, chiefly because it is not necessary for Officer Montgomery to respond to visitors while on a break
    B. *incorrect*, chiefly because Officer Montgomery should have ejected the visitor from the facility
    C. *correct*, chiefly because special officers should ignore insults
    D. *incorrect*, chiefly because visitors should not be allowed to ridicule authority figures such as special officers

12. While patrolling the facility parking lot, Officer 12.___
Klausner sees an unoccupied car parked in front of a fire
hydrant. Officer Klausner writes out a summons for a
parking violation and places it on the windshield of the
car. As the Officer begins to walk away, the owner of
the car spots the summons on the windshield and runs over
to the car. The car owner is furious at getting the
summons, confronts the Officer, and curses him loudly.
In this situation, Officer Klausner should
   A. curse back at the car owner just as loudly
   B. push him out of the way and resume patrol
   C. calmly explain to him the nature of the violation
   D. return all the insults but in a calm tone

Question 13.

DIRECTIONS: Question 13 is to be answered SOLELY on the basis of
the following information.

Special Officers are permitted to give only general information
about social services. They shall not provide advice concerning
specific procedures.

13. Special Officer Lynn King is on post near the Medicaid 13.___
Office in the Manhattan Income Maintenance Center.
While Officer King is on post, a client approaches her
and asks which forms must be filled out in order to
apply for Medicaid benefits. Officer King tells the
client that she cannot help him and directs the client
to the Medicaid Office.
In this situation, Officer King's response to the client's
question is
   A. *correct*, chiefly because Officer King's duties do
      not include providing any information to clients
   B. *incorrect*, chiefly because Officer King should have
      provided as much specific information as possible
      to the client
   C. *correct*, chiefly because Officer King may not advise
      clients on social services procedures
   D. *incorrect*, chiefly because Officer King should know
      which forms are used in the facility

Question 14.

DIRECTIONS: Question 14 is to be answered SOLELY on the basis of
the following information.

Security Officers must request that visitors and clients show
identification and inspect that identification before allowing them
to enter restricted areas in the facility.

14. Security Officer Crane is assigned to a fixed post outside Commissioner Maxwell's office, which is a restricted area. A visitor approaches Officer Crane's desk and states that he is Robert Maxwell and has an appointment with the Commissioner, who is his brother. Officer Crane checks the appointment book, verifies that Robert Maxwell has an appointment with the Commissioner, and allows the visitor to enter the office.
In this situation, Officer Crane's action in allowing the visitor admittance to the Commissioner's office is
   A. *correct*, chiefly because he verified that Robert Maxwell had an appointment with the Commissioner
   B. *incorrect*, chiefly because all visitors must show identification before entering restricted areas
   C. *correct*, chiefly because it would insult the Commissioner's brother if he was asked to show identification
   D. *incorrect*, chiefly because he should have called the Commissioner to verify that he has a brother

Question 15.

DIRECTIONS: Question 15 is to be answered SOLELY on the basis of the following information.

While on duty, a Special Officer must give his rank, name, and shield number to any person who requests it.

15. Special Officer Karen Mitchell is assigned to patrol an area in the North Bronx Service Facility. While on patrol, Officer Mitchell observes a visitor asking other clients in the lobby for money. Upon investigation, she determines that the visitor has no official business in the facility and asks the visitor to leave the premises. The individual says that he will leave but demands to know Officer Mitchell's name and shield number.
In response to the visitor's demand, Officer Mitchell should
   A. give the individual her name and shield number
   B. inform him that he can only obtain that information from her supervisor
   C. ignore his demand and resume her patrol
   D. tell the visitor that she will issue a summons to him if he keeps bothering her

Question 16.

DIRECTIONS: Question 16 is to be answered SOLELY on the basis of the following information.

A member of the Security Staff must follow guidelines for providing information to reporters concerning official facility business. Special Officers shall not be interviewed, nor make public speeches or statements pertaining to official business unless authorized. Security Staff must receive authorization from the Office of Public Affairs before speaking to reporters on any matters pertaining to official facility business.

16. You are a Special Officer in a Men's Shelter. A reporter approaches you as you are leaving the building. The reporter requests that you give an insider's view on conditions in the shelter. He assures you that you will remain anonymous.
You should tell the reporter that you
   A. must obtain permission from your immediate supervisor before giving any interviews
   B. will be more than happy to provide him with information concerning conditions in the shelter
   C. must receive authorization from the Office of Public Affairs before giving any interviews
   D. may not give him any information, but that your supervisor will be able to provide him with the requested information.

Questions 17-21.

DIRECTIONS: Questions 17 through 21 are to be answered SOLELY on the basis of the following information.

During their tours, Security Officers are required to transmit and receive information and commands over two-way portable radios from other security staff members. Officers use a numbered code to transmit information over the radio. For example, an officer who calls *10-13* into his radio communicates to other officers and supervisors that he is in need of assistance. Assume that the code numbers shown below along with their specified meanings are those used by Special Officers.

Code	Meaning
10-01	Call your command
10-02	Report to your command
10-03	Call Dispatcher
10-04	Acknowledgment
10-05	Repeat message
10-06	Stand-by
10-07	Verify
10-08	Respond to specified area and advise
10-10	Investigate
10-13	Officer needs help
10-20	Robbery in progress
10-21	Burglary in progress
10-22	Larceny in progress
10-24	Assault in progress
10-30	Robbery has occurred
10-31	Burglary has occurred
10-34	Assault has occurred
10-40	Unusual incident
10-41	Vehicle accident
10-42	Traffic or parking problem
10-43	Electrical problem
10-50	Dispute or noise
10-52	Disorderly person/group

Code	Meaning
10-60	Ambulance needed
10-61	Police Department assistance required
10-64	Fire alarm
10-70	Arrived at scene
10-71	Arrest
10-72	Unfounded
10-73	Condition corrected
10-74	Resuming normal duties

17. Officer Cramer is patrolling Parking Lot A when he receives a radio message from Sergeant Wong. Sergeant Wong directs Officer Cramer to respond to Parking Lot B to investigate a reported traffic problem. Upon arriving at Parking Lot B, Officer Cramer observes a vehicle blocking a loading dock so that a delivery truck cannot gain access to the dock. After notification is made to the owner of the vehicle, the vehicle is moved, allowing the delivery truck to gain access to the loading dock. Which of the following should Officer Cramer use to BEST report the events that occurred back to Sergeant Wong?
    A. 10-72, 10-41, 10-73
    B. 10-70, 10-42, 10-73
    C. 10-70, 10-41, 10-74
    D. 10-72, 10-42, 10-74

17.___

18. Officer Garret receives a message of *10-24, 10-10* on his radio from his supervisor, Sergeant Gomez. Officer Garret responds to the scene and later sends Sergeant Gomez the following message in response: *10-70, 10-72, 10-74.* Which of the following events are reported by use of those codes?
Sergeant Gomez ordered Officer Garret to investigate an assault
    A. in progress. Officer Garret arrived at the scene, discovered that the report was unfounded, and resumed normal duties.
    B. that had occurred. Officer Garret arrived at the scene, made an arrest, and then resumed normal duties.
    C. that had occurred. Officer Garret arrived at the scene and discovered that the report was unfounded and resumed normal duties.
    D. in progress. Officer Garret arrived at the scene, made an arrest, and then resumed normal duties.

18.___

19. Officer Torres is patrolling the grounds of his facility when he receives a radio message from Sergeant Washington. In response to the radio message, Officer Torres goes to the facility's parking lot and issues a summons to a vehicle blocking an ambulance entrance.
The radio message that Officer Torres received from Sergeant Washington is 10-10,
    A. 10-21   B. 10-40   C. 10-42   D. 10-43

19.___

20. Officer Oxford transmits the following codes by radio to Sergeant Joseph: *10-20, 10-13*. The response that Officer Oxford receives from Sergeant Joseph on her radio is *10-04*.
Which one of the following events are reported by the use of those codes?
Officer Oxford informed Sergeant Joseph that
   A. a robbery was in progress and that she needs assistance, and Sergeant Joseph acknowledged her message
   B. an assault was in progress and that she wants him to respond to the area, and Sergeant Joseph acknowledged her message
   C. a burglary was in progress and that someone must investigate, and Sergeant Joseph responded that he is standing by
   D. a larceny was in progress and that she needs him to call a dispatcher. Sergeant Joseph reports this incident to his command.

20.___

21. While on patrol, Officer Robinson observes that the hall lights in Wing *B* are flickering on and off. Officer Robinson calls the Maintenance Office and a maintenance worker responds and corrects the problem.
The radio code that Officer Robinson should transmit to his supervisor to report this incident is
   A. 10-06, 10-08
   B. 10-40, 10-64
   C. 10-43, 10-73
   D. 10-61, 10-07

21.___

Question 22.

DIRECTIONS: Question 22 is to be answered SOLELY on the basis of the following information.

The two-way portable radios used by Security or Special Officers to communicate with other security staff members are to be used for official business only. In addition, when transmitting official business, transmission time (time spent transmitting information to other staff) should be kept to a minimum.

22. During his tour, Special Officer Banks calls Sergeant Gates in the patrolroom over the radio and asks if his wife, Alice Banks, had telephoned. Sergeant Gates tells Officer Banks that his wife has not called. Officer Banks then requests that Sergeant Gates notify him as soon as his wife calls because he is expecting an important message concerning his family.
In this situation, Officer Banks' use of his radio is
   A. *appropriate*, chiefly because his transmission time was not excessive
   B. *inappropriate*, chiefly because he should have made the transmission on his break
   C. *appropriate*, chiefly because his transmission concerned an important family matter
   D. *inappropriate*, chiefly because radios are to be used for official business only

22.___

Question 23.

DIRECTIONS: Question 23 is to be answered SOLELY on the basis of the following information.

Special Officers are responsible for monitoring and responding to radio messages, even if the officer is on meal break, performing clerical duties, or away from his post for other reasons. An officer shall answer radio messages directed to him during his tour.

23. Officer Lewis is chatting with friends in the cafeteria while on her scheduled meal break when she receives a radio message from Sergeant Baker. Sergeant Baker informs Officer Lewis that trouble has broken out at Location A and directs her to report to Location A immediately to assist the officers on the scene. Officer Lewis leaves the cafeteria immediately and reports to the scene.
Officer Lewis' action in response to Sergeant Baker's radio message is
   A. *correct*, chiefly because Officer Lewis is responsible for responding to all radio messages
   B. *incorrect*, chiefly because Officer Lewis is on meal break and therefore *off-duty*
   C. *correct*, chiefly because Officer Lewis was not doing anything important during her meal break
   D. *incorrect*, chiefly because the situation was not declared a *total emergency*

23.____

Question 24.

DIRECTIONS: Question 24 is to be answered SOLELY on the basis of the following information.

Special Officers must immediately report to their supervisor any incident or condition in the facility that may cause danger or inconvenience to the public.

24. Special Officer Scott is patrolling a small, crowded waiting room in his facility when two male clients start arguing with each other, shoving chairs around and frightening the other clients. Officer Scott intervenes in the argument, issues summonses for Disorderly Conduct to the individuals involved in the dispute, and escorts them off the premises. Officer Scott then records the incident in his memo book and resumes patrol.
In this situation, the FIRST action that Officer Scott should have taken when he observed the argument start between the two men is to
   A. call for help from Special Officers on nearby posts to restrain the men who were fighting
   B. report the incident to his supervisor immediately

24.____

C. attempt to separate the men who were fighting in order to stop the fight
D. evacuate the waiting room so that innocent bystanders would not be injured

Question 25.

DIRECTIONS: Question 25 is to be answered SOLELY on the basis of the following information.

An Officer on duty in a facility must remain on post until properly relieved. If not properly relieved as scheduled, he must notify his immediate supervisor by radio of this fact and follow the supervisor's instructions.

25. Officer Clough is working on an 8:00 A.M. to 4:00 P.M. tour. Officer Clough is to be relieved at 4:00 P.M. by Security Officer Crandall, who works the 4:00 P.M. to 12:00 Midnight shift. However, as of 4:15 P.M., Officer Crandall has not appeared to relieve Officer Clough, so Officer Clough leaves his post to find Officer Crandall. In this situation, Officer Clough's action is

A. *correct*, chiefly because his tour was over and he wanted to go home
B. *incorrect*, chiefly because he should have notified his supervisor of Officer Crandall's failure to relieve him
C. *correct*, chiefly because Officer Clough is attempting to locate Officer Crandall so that the post will be covered
D. *incorrect*, chiefly because Officer Clough should have left his post as soon as his tour ended rather than working any overtime

25.___

Questions 26-28.

DIRECTIONS: Questions 26 through 28 are to be answered SOLELY on the basis of the following information.

A summons is a written notice that a person is accused of violating a code or regulation. Special Officers have the authority to issue summonses to individuals for on-premises parking or traffic violations, or violations of the City Administrative Code. Summonses for violations of the Penal Law, such as for Disorderly Conduct, may also be issued.

The following is a list of types of summonses issued for violations and their descriptions:

Type of Summons	Description of Violation
Class A	Parking in fire lanes
Class A	Parking in space reserved for the handicapped
Class A	Vehicle blocking driveway
Class B	Disobeying stop sign

Type of Summons	Description of Violation
Class C	Disorderly Conduct
Class C	Harassment
Environmental Control Board	Smoking Violations
Environmental Control Board	Public Health Code

26. While on patrol, Special Officer Gladys Jones observes a parked car that is blocking a driveway.
    She should issue a summons for a violation which is a
    A. Class A type   B. Class B type
    C. Class C type   D. Environmental Control Board

27. A man drives up to a facility, parks his car in a fire lane, and quickly runs inside the facility. An attempt to follow and locate the man is unsuccessful.
    Which one of the following is the type of summons that the Special Officer on duty should issue?
    A. Class A   B. Class B
    C. Class C   D. Environmental Control Board

28. While on patrol, Special Officer Mason observes a visitor smoking a cigarette in an area where smoking is prohibited. Officer Mason asks the visitor to stop smoking and shows him the *No Smoking* sign posted. The visitor refuses to comply.
    Officer Mason should issue which type of summons?
    A. Class A   B. Class B
    C. Class C   D. Environmental Control Board

Questions 29-31.

DIRECTIONS: Questions 29 through 31 are to be answered SOLELY on the basis of the following information and the Summons Form and Fact Pattern.

Special Officers must complete a summons form by filling in the appropriate information. A completed summons must include the name and address of the accused; license or other identification number; vehicle identification; the section number of the code, regulation, or law violated; a brief description of the violation; any scheduled fine; information about the time and place of occurrence; and the name, rank, and signature of the Special Officer issuing the summons.

The information listed on the Summons Form may or may not be correct.

13 (#1)

SUMMONS FORM

LINE:	NOTICE OF VIOLATION No. 5 56784989		THE PEOPLE OF THE STATE OF NEW YORK VS._____	
1			OPERATOR PRESENT NO (YES) REFUSED ID	
	LAST NAME	FIRST NAME		MIDDLE INITIAL
2	Tucker	James		T
	STREET ADDRESS			
3	205 E. 53rd Street			
	CITY (AS SHOWN ON LICENSE)			
4	Brooklyn, NY 11234			
	DRIVER LICENSE OR IDENTIFICATION NO.	STATE	CLASS	DATE EXPIRES
5	J-7156907834	NY	5	1/12/91
	SEX	DATE OF BIRTH		
6	M	1/12/50		
	LICENSE PLATE NO.	STATE	DATE EXPIRES	OPERATOR OWN VEHICLE?
7	CVR-632	NY	8/12/90	(YES) NO
	BODY TYPE	MAKE		COLOR
8	Sedan	Dodge		Green
	THE PERSON DESCRIBED ABOVE IS CHARGED AS FOLLOWS:			
	ISSUE TIME	DATE OF OFFENSE	TIME FIRST OBSERVED	COUNTY
9	9:30 A.M.	2/5/90	9:28 A.M.	Kings
	PLACE OF OCCURRENCE			PRECINCT
10	451 Clarkson Ave., Brooklyn, NY			71st
	IN VIOLATION OF	CODE	LAW	
11	SECTION 81-B	40	New York State Traffic Regulation	
	DESCRIPTION OF VIOLATION			
12	Vehicle parked in front of a fire hydrant			
	SCHEDULED FINE			
13	$10 $15 $20 $25 $30 ($40) Other $____			
	RANK/NAME OF ISSUING OFFICER		SIGNATURE OF ISSUING OFFICER	
14	Special Officer Joseph Robbins		Joseph Robbins	

FACT PATTERN

On February 5, 1990, at 9:28 A.M., Special Officer Joseph Robbins is patrolling the grounds of the Brooklyn Hills Income Maintenance Center, located at 451 Clarkson Ave., Brooklyn, NY, when he observes an unoccupied parked vehicle blocking a fire hydrant near the facility's entrance. As Officer Robbins begins to write up a summons for the violation, James Tucker, the owner of the vehicle, emerges from the facility and comes over. While getting in his car, he asks why he is getting a summons. Officer Robbins explains to Mr. Tucker that he is in violation of traffic regulations pertaining to access to fire hydrants and asks him for identification. Mr. Tucker gives Officer Robbins his driver's license, showing the following information:

    Name: Tucker, James T.
    Address: 205 E. 53rd Street, Brooklyn, NY 11234
    Date of Birth: January 12, 1950
    Driver's License: J-7156907894
    Driver License
      Expiration Date: January 12, 1991
    Class: 5

29. The *place of occurrence* of the violation described in the Fact Pattern is on line _____ of the Summons Form.
   A. 2   B. 3   C. 8   D. 10

30. Which one of the following lines on the Summons Form shows information that does NOT agree with information given in the Fact Pattern?
   A. 1   B. 2   C. 4   D. 5

31. Which of the following is the date on which the violation occurred?
   A. 1/12/90   B. 2/5/90   C. 8/12/90   D. 1/12/91

32. Following are two sentences which may or may not be written in correct English:
   I. Two clients assaulted the officer.
   II. The van is illegally parked.
   Which one of the following statements is CORRECT?
   A. Only Sentence I is written in correct English.
   B. Only Sentence II is written in correct English.
   C. Sentences I and II are both written in correct English.
   D. Neither Sentence I nor Sentence II is written in correct English.

33. Following are two sentences which may or may not be written in correct English:
   I. Security Officer Rollo escorted the visitor to the patrolroom.
   II. Two entry were made in the facility logbook.
   Which one of the following statements is CORRECT?
   A. Only Sentence I is written in correct English.
   B. Only Sentence II is written in correct English.
   C. Sentences I and II are both written in correct English.
   D. Neither Sentence I nor Sentence II is written in correct English.

34. Following are two sentences which may or may not be written in correct English:
   I. Officer McElroy putted out a small fire in the wastepaper basket.
   II. Special Officer Janssen told the visitor where he could obtained a pass.
   Which one of the following statements is CORRECT?
   A. Only Sentence I is written in correct English.
   B. Only Sentence II is written in correct English.
   C. Sentences I and II are both written in correct English.
   D. Neither Sentence I nor Sentence II are written in correct English.

35. Following are two sentences which may or may not be written in correct English:
   I. Security Officer Warren observed a broken window while he was on his post in Hallway C.
   II. The worker reported that two typewriters had been stoled from the office.

   Which one of the following statements is CORRECT?
   A. Only Sentence I is written in correct English.
   B. Only Sentence II is written in correct English.
   C. Sentences I and II are both written in correct English.
   D. Neither Sentence I nor Sentence II is written in correct English.

KEY (CORRECT ANSWERS)

1. C	11. C	21. C	31. B
2. A	12. C	22. D	32. C
3. D	13. C	23. A	33. A
4. B	14. B	24. B	34. D
5. C	15. A	25. B	35. A
6. B	16. C	26. A	
7. D	17. B	27. A	
8. A	18. A	28. D	
9. B	19. C	29. D	
10. B	20. A	30. D	

TEST 2

DIRECTIONS: Each question or incomplete statement is followed by several suggested answers or completions. Select the one that BEST answers the question or completes the statement. *PRINT THE LETTER OF THE CORRECT ANSWER IN THE SPACE AT THE RIGHT.*

Questions 1-5.

DIRECTIONS: Questions 1 through 5 are to be answered SOLELY on the basis of the following information.

Special Officers have the power to arrest members of the public who commit crimes in violation of the Penal Law. Assume that certain classes of crimes covered by various sections of the Penal Law are described below. Special Officers must be able to apply this information when making an arrest in order to accurately determine the type of crime that has been committed.

Crime	Class of Crime	Description of Crime	Section
Petit Larceny	A Misdemeanor	Stealing property worth up to $250	155.25
Grand Larceny 3rd Degree	E Felony	Stealing property worth more than $250	155.30
Grand Larceny 2nd Degree	D Felony	Stealing property worth more than $1,500	155.35
Grand Larceny 1st Degree	C Felony	Stealing property worth any amount of money while making a person fear injury or damage to property	155.40
Assault 3rd Degree	A Misdemeanor	Injuring a person	120.00
Assault 2nd Degree	D Felony	1. Seriously injuring a person; or 2. Injuring an officer of the law	120.05
Assault 1st Degree	C Felony	Seriously injuring a person using a deadly or dangerous weapon	120.10
Disorderly Conduct	Violation	1. Engages in fighting or threatening behavior; or 2. Makes unreasonable noise	240.20
Robbery 3rd Degree	D Felony	Stealing property by force	160.05
Robbery 2nd Degree	C Felony	1. Stealing property by force with the help of another person; or 2. Stealing property by force and injuring any person	160.10
Robbery 1st Degree	B Felony	Stealing property by force and seriously injuring the owner of property	160.15

1. Which one of the following crimes is considered to be Class *A* Misdemeanor?
   A. Grand Larceny - 3rd Degree
   B. Grand Larceny - 2nd Degree
   C. Assault - 3rd Degree
   D. Assault - 2nd Degree

2. Which one of the following crimes is considered to be Class *B* Felony?
   A. Robbery - 2nd Degree
   B. Robbery - 1st Degree
   C. Grand Larceny - 3rd Degree
   D. Grand Larceny - 2nd Degree

3. A worker at a facility reports that a typewriter worth $400 has been stolen from her office.
   Which one of the following is the type of crime that has been committed?
   A. Grand Larceny - 3rd Degree
   B. Grand Larceny - 2nd Degree
   C. Grand Larceny - 1st Degree
   D. Petit Larceny

4. A visitor at a facility begins yelling very loudly at a receptionist and shakes his fist at her. The visitor refuses to stop yelling when an officer tries to calm him down, and he shakes his fist at the officer.
   Which one of the following is the type of crime that occurred?
   A. Assault - 3rd Degree   B. Assault - 2nd Degree
   C. Assault - 1st Degree   D. Disorderly Conduct

5. An officer has apprehended and arrested a visitor who was attempting to leave the facility with a radio he had stolen from an office. The radio is worth $100.
   Under which one of the following sections of the Penal Law should the visitor be charged?
   Section
   A. 155.25   B. 155.30   C. 155.35   D. 155.40

Questions 6-12.

DIRECTIONS: Questions 6 through 12 are to be answered SOLELY on the basis of the Arrest Report Form and Incident Report shown on the following page. These reports were submitted by Special Officer John Clark, Shield #512, to his supervisor, Sergeant Joseph Lewis, Shield #818, of the North Bay Health Clinic

Special Officers are required to complete both an Arrest Report Form and an Incident Report whenever an unusual incident or an arrest occurs. The Arrest Report Form provides detailed information regarding the victim and the person arrested, along with a brief description of the incident.

The Incident Report provides a detailed description of the incident. Both reports include the following information: WHO was involved in the incident, including witnesses; WHAT happened and HOW it happened; WHERE and WHEN the incident occurred; and WHY the incident occurred.

ARREST REPORT FORM

ARREST INFORMATION	(1)	TIME OF OCCURRENCE 11:15 A.M.	DATE OF OCCURRENCE February 1, 1990	DAY OF WEEK Monday	
INFORMATION ABOUT VICTIM	(2)	VICTIM'S NAME Darlene Kirk		ADDRESS 7855 Cruger St., Bronx, NY 10488	
	(3)	SEX F / DATE OF BIRTH 9/3/60	RACE White	HOME TELEPHONE # 212-733-3462	SOCIAL SECURITY # 245-63-0772
INFORMATION ABOUT PERSON ARRESTED	(4)	NAME OF PERSON ARRESTED Elsie Gardner		ADDRESS 2447 Southern Pkway, Bronx, NY 10467	
	(5)	SEX F / DATE OF BIRTH 7/9/65	RACE White	HOME TELEPHONE # 212-513-7029	SOCIAL SECURITY # 244-08-0569
	(6)	HEIGHT 5'5" / WEIGHT 135 lbs.	HAIR COLOR Brown	CLOTHING Black coat/red pants	
DESCRIPTION OF CRIME	(7)	SECTION OF PENAL LAW 120.00		TYPE OF CRIME Assault - 3rd Degree	
	(8)	TIME OF ARREST 11:35 A.M.	DATE OF ARREST 2/1/90	LOCATION OF ARREST 635 Bay Avenue Bronx, NY	
	(9)	DESCRIPTION OF INCIDENT The defendant, Elsie Gardner, struck the victim after the victim requested that Ms. Gardner stop smoking in a "NO SMOKING" area. Two witnesses verified the victim's account of the incident.			
INFORMATION ABOUT ARRESTING OFFICER	(10)	REPORTING OFFICER'S SIGNATURE *John Clark*		NAME PRINTED John Clark	
	(11)	RANK Special Officer	SHIELD NUMBER 512		

INCIDENT REPORT

(1) At 11:15 A.M. on February 1, 1990, I was directed by Sergeant Mark Lewis via two-way radio to report to the Nutrition Clinic on the 4th Floor to investigate a disturbance. (2) Special Officer Anna Colon, Shield #433, was directed to assist me. (3) At 11:16 A.M., Officer Colon and I arrived at the Health Clinic and observed a patient, Elsie Gardner, repeatedly strike Health Clinic receptionist Darlene Kirk about the head and neck. (4) Officer Colon restrained Ms. Gardner while I placed handcuffs on her wrists. (5) Ms. Kirk complained that her neck felt sore. (6) After being examined by Dr. Stone, Ms. Kirk told us that Ms. Gardner entered the Health Clinic at approximately 11:10 A.M. and lit a cigarette in the waiting area. (7) At 11:20 A.M., Dr. Paul Stone examined Ms. Kirk. (8) Ms. Kirk explained to Ms. Gardner that smoking was not allowed in the Health Clinic and showed her the *NO SMOKING* signs posted on the walls. (9) Ms. Gardner ignored Ms. Kirk, and then grew very abusive and attacked her when

Ms. Kirk insisted that she stop smoking. (10) Two witnesses, patients Edna Manning of 8937 4th Ave., Bronx, NY, and John Schultz of 357 149th Street, Bronx, NY, gave the same account of the incident as Ms. Kirk. (11) At 11:30 A.M., I read the prisoner her rights and placed her under arrest for violation of Penal Law Section 120.00 - Assault 3rd Degree. (12) At 11:35 A.M., I notified the 86th Precinct of Ms. Gardner's arrest and arranged for the transportation of the prisoner to the precinct. (13) At 11:40 A.M., Officer Colon escorted Ms. Gardner from the Nutrition Clinic to the patrolroom. (14) At 11:55 A.M., Police Officers Cranford, Shield #658, and Wargo, Shield #313, arrived at the facility to transport the prisoner to the precinct. (15) Officer Gray, Shield #936, assumed my post while I reported to the patrolroom to complete the necessary forms concerning the arrest.

6. At what time did Sergeant Lewis inform Officer John Clark of the disturbance in the Nutrition Clinic?
   _____ A.M.
   A. 11:00   B. 11:15   C. 11:16   D. 11:20

7. According to the Arrest Report and the Incident Report, how many witnesses gave the same account of the incident as Ms. Kirk?
   A. 1   B. 2   C. 3   D. 4

8. What information on the Arrest Report is NOT included in the Incident Report?
   A. Date of Occurrence
   B. Victim's address
   C. Section of the Penal Law violated
   D. Assault 3rd Degree

9. Which sentence in the Incident Report is out of order in terms of the sequence of events?
   A. 3   B. 6   C. 11   D. 12

10. According to the Incident Report, at 11:40 A.M. Ms. Gardner was
    A. escorted to the patrolroom
    B. transported to the 86th Precinct
    C. examined by Dr. Paul Stone
    D. giving an account of the incident to Special Officers Clark and Colon

11. According to the Incident Report, which one of the following officers relieved Officer Clark?
    Officer
    A. Colon   B. Cranford   C. Wargo   D. Gray

12. Which section of the Arrest Report contains information that does NOT agree with Sentence 11 of the Incident Report?
    Section
    A. 1   B. 7   C. 8   D. 9

Question 13.

DIRECTIONS: Question 13 is to be answered SOLELY on the basis of the following information.

A Security Officer must investigate any complaint or incident which occurs in the facility, whether he considers it is major or minor. The Officer must also interview the person(s) involved in the incident in order to complete the necessary forms and reports.

13. Ms. Peters, a clerical worker at the facility, complains to Officer Tynan that a pen set, which had been given to her as a gift, was missing from her desk. She tells Officer Tynan that she knows the pen set was on her desk the previous day because she was using it for her work. Officer Tynan informs Ms. Peters that there is nothing he can do since the pen set was personal property and not facility property.
In this situation, Officer Tynan's response to Ms. Peters is
    A. *correct*, chiefly because the pen set should not have been left out on a desk where it could be stolen
    B. *incorrect*, chiefly because a complaint of a loss of theft should be investigated and recorded
    C. *correct*, chiefly because Special Officers are only required to investigate a loss or theft of facility property
    D. *incorrect*, chiefly because Ms. Peters' work required use of the pen set

13.___

Question 14.

DIRECTIONS: Question 14 is to be answered SOLELY on the basis of the following information.

Assume that Security Officers are responsible for recording in a personal memobook all of their routine and non-routine activities and occurrences for each tour of duty. Before starting a tour of duty, a Security Officer must enter in his personal memobook the date, tour, and assigned post. An entry shall be made to record each absence from duty, such as a regular day off, sick leave, annual leave, or holiday. During each tour, a Security Officer shall enter a full and accurate record of duties performed, changes in post assignment, absences from post, and the reason for each absence, and all other patrol business.

14. Security Officer Ella Lewis is assigned to Gotham Center Facility, where she works Monday through Friday on a 9:00 A.M. to 5:00 P.M. tour. Officer Lewis' regular days off are Saturday and Sunday. Officer Lewis worked on Wednesday, November 25, 1990. She was absent on Thursday, November 26, 1990, for Thanksgiving Holiday, and on Friday, November 27, 1990, for annual leave.

14.___

According to the information given above, which of the following entries is the FIRST entry that Officer Lewis should record in her memobook when she returns to work on November 30, 1990?
  A. Saturday, 11/28/90 and Sunday, 11/29/90 - Regular days off
  B. Friday, 11/27/90 - Sick Leave
  C. Monday, 11/30/90 - On duty
  D. Thursday, 11/26/90 - Thanksgiving Holiday

Questions 15-16.

DIRECTIONS: Questions 15 and 16 are to be answered SOLELY on the basis of the following entries recorded by Security Officer Angela Russo in her memobook.

Date: January 8, 1990
Tour: 8:00 A.M. to 4:00 P.M.
Weather: Sunny and clear

7:30 Reported to B Command for Roll Call. Assigned to Post #2, C Building Emergency Room Corridor by Sergeant Robert Floyd.
  Break: 9:30 A.M.
  Meal: 1:30 P.M.
  Radio: #701

7:40 Arrived at Post #2 and relieved Special Officer Johnson, Shield #593.

7:45 On patrol - Post #2.

8:00 Post #2 - All secure at this time; conditions normal.

8:30 Fire Alarm Box 5-3-1 rings on 3rd Floor South in C Building. Upon arrival, Office Worker Molly Lewis reported that a wastepaper basket was on fire. Used fire extinguisher to put out fire.

8:50 Condition corrected; Incident Report prepared and submitted to Sergeant Floyd in B Command.

8:55 Resumed patrol of Post #2.

9:30 Relieved for break by Officer Tucker.

9:50 Resumed patrol of Post #2.

10:10 Disorderly person reported by Clinic Director Lila Jones on Ward C-32; Officer Bailey and myself responded. Clinic Director Jones informed officers that visitor Bradley Manna, male white, 19 years of age, 2 Park Place, Brooklyn, NY, is drunk and has been shouting insults to Clinic staff.

10:30 Condition corrected; Visitor Bradley Manna escorted off premises. B Command notified of incident.

10:40	Resumed patrol of Post #2.
11:40	Post #2 - All secure at this time.
12:40	Post #2 - All secure at this time.

15. The name of the Clinic Director who reported a disorderly person is
    A. Molly Lewis
    B. Bradley Manna
    C. Lila Jones
    D. Robert Floyd

16. Which of the following sets of officers responded to the report of a disorderly person on Ward C-32? Officers
    A. Johnson and Bailey
    B. Russo and Tucker
    C. Johnson and Tucker
    D. Russo and Bailey

17. Security Officer Mace is completing an entry in her memobook. The entry has the following five sentences:
    1. I observed the defendant removing a radio from a facility vehicle.
    2. I placed the defendant under arrest and escorted him to the patrolroom.
    3. I was patrolling the facility parking lot.
    4. I asked the defendant to show identification.
    5. I determined that the defendant was not authorized to remove the radio.
    The MOST logical order for these sentences to be entered in Officer Mace's memobook is
    A. 1, 3, 2, 4, 5
    B. 2, 5, 4, 1, 3
    C. 3, 1, 4, 5, 2
    D. 4, 5, 2, 1, 3

18. Security Officer Riley is completing an entry in his memobook. The entry has the following five sentences:
    1. Anna Jones admitted that she stole Mary Green's wallet.
    2. I approached the women and asked them who they were and why they were arguing.
    3. I arrested Anna Jones for stealing Mary Green's wallet.
    4. They identified themselves and Mary Green accused Anna Jones of stealing her wallet.
    5. I was in the lobby area when I observed two women arguing about a wallet.
    The MOST logical order for these sentences to be entered in Officer Riley's memobook is
    A. 2, 4, 1, 3, 5
    B. 3, 1, 4, 5, 2
    C. 4, 1, 5, 2, 3
    D. 5, 2, 4, 1, 3

19. Assume that Security Officer John Ryan is completing an entry in his memobook. The entry has the following five sentences:
   1. I then cleared the immediate area of visitors and staff.
   2. I noticed smoke coming from a broom closet outside Room A71.
   3. Sergeant Mueller arrived with other officers to assist in clearing the area.
   4. Upon investigation, I determined the smoke was due to burning material in the broom closet.
   5. I pulled the corridor fire alarm and notified Sergeant Mueller of the fire.

   The MOST logical order for these sentences to be entered in Officer Ryan's memobook is
   A. 2, 3, 4, 5, 1
   B. 2, 4, 5, 1, 3
   C. 4, 1, 2, 3, 5
   D. 5, 3, 2, 1, 4

20. Security Officer Hernandez is completing an entry in his memobook. The entry has the following five sentences:
   1. I asked him to leave the premises immediately.
   2. A visitor complained that there was a strange man loitering in Clinic B hallway.
   3. I went to investigate and saw a man dressed in rags sitting on the floor of the hallway.
   4. As he walked out, he started yelling that he had no place to go.
   5. I asked to see identification, but he said that he did not have any.

   The MOST logical order for these sentences to be entered in Officer Hernandez's memobook is
   A. 2, 3, 5, 1, 4
   B. 3, 1, 2, 4, 5
   C. 4, 1, 5, 2, 3
   D. 3, 1, 5, 2, 4

21. Officer Hogan is completing an entry in his memobook. The entry has the following five sentences:
   1. When the fighting had stopped, I transmitted a message requesting medical assistance for Mr. Perkins.
   2. Special Officer Manning assisted me in stopping the fight.
   3. When I arrived at the scene, I saw a client, Adam Finley strike a facility employee, Peter Perkins.
   4. As I attempted to break up the fight, Special Officer Manning came on the scene.
   5. I received a radio message from Sergeant Valez to investigate a possible fight in progress in the waiting room.

   The MOST logical order for these sentences to be entered in Officer Hogan's memobook is
   A. 2, 1, 4, 5, 3
   B. 3, 5, 2, 4, 1
   C. 4, 5, 3, 1, 2
   D. 5, 3, 4, 2, 1

Questions 22-23.

DIRECTIONS: Questions 22 and 23 are to be answered SOLELY on the basis of the following information.

Assume that Security Officers may be assigned to the facility patrolroom and must follow the guidelines below in documenting all routine and non-routine activities and occurrences in the facility logbook.

At the beginning of each tour of duty, the Security Officer responsible for entering information in the logbook must transfer from the Roll Call Sheet to the logbook a list of all security staff personnel assigned to that tour. This list is to be entered in order of the rank of the security staff member. All other entries in the facility logbook shall be recorded in chronological order, in blue or black ink, and be neat and legible.

22. When recording the list of security staff personnel assigned to a tour, that entry shall be made in
    A. chronological order
    B. order of rank of security staff
    C. alphabetical order
    D. order of arrival at facility

23. A Security Officer has transmitted notification to the patrolroom that he has just issued a summons. The Security Officer responsible for documenting occurrences in the patrolroom logbook should record the information
    A. in red ink, immediately following the previous entry
    B. on a new page under the heading *Summonses Reported*
    C. in blue or black ink immediately following the previous entry
    D. on the last page of the logbook where it can be easily found

Question 24.

DIRECTIONS: Question 24 is to be answered SOLELY on the basis of the following information.

Assume that whenever a Security Officer is to begin a leave of absence, long-term sick leave, or other type of leave having an anticipated length of ten days or more, the officer shall surrender his or her security shield to his supervisor, who shall immediately forward it to Security Headquarters.

24. Two male clients were fighting in the waiting room of North End Hospital. Officer Gary Klott attempted to separate them and became involved in the altercation. Officer Klott sustained an injury to the right eye and was examined by a physician. The physician directed Officer Klott to stay home for a recovery period of 12 days.

In this situation, Officer Klott should
A. surrender his shield to his supervisor
B. safeguard his shield in a safe place at home while he is recovering
C. surrender his shield to the physician
D. safeguard his shield with his uniform in his locker at the facility while he is recovering

Question 25.

DIRECTIONS: Question 25 is to be answered SOLELY on the basis of the following information.

Assume that Security Officers are required to follow certain procedures when on post at a restricted area of a facility. They must inspect the identification of employees and passes of visitors, as well as all bags and packages carried by individuals who wish to enter the restricted area.

25. Security Officer Stevens is assigned to a post at the Intensive Care Unit of Park View Hospital, a restricted area. Officer Stevens is responsible for inspecting identification and passes, as well as all bags and packages carried by individuals who want to enter the Unit. He sees Mr. Craig approach. He knows Mr. Craig's wife is a patient in the Unit. Officer Stevens has seen Mr. Craig visit his wife every day for the past four days. Mr. Craig brings a small duffel bag filled with magazines each time he comes. Today, Officer Stevens checks Mr. Craig's visitor's pass but lets Mr. Craig enter the Unit without checking his duffel bag.
In this situation, Officer Stevens' action is
A. *correct*, chiefly because he has checked to see that Mr. Craig has a visitor's pass
B. *incorrect*, chiefly because all packages and bags must be inspected before anyone is allowed to enter a restricted area
C. *correct*, chiefly because he is familiar with Mr. Craig and knows that he only carries magazines in his duffel bag
D. *incorrect*, chiefly because Mr. Craig should not be allowed to carry a bag or package into a restricted area of the facility

25.___

Question 26.

DIRECTIONS: Question 26 is to be answered SOLELY on the basis of the following information.

Assume that Special Officers must safeguard evidence in cases involving firearms. Special Officers must mark recovered bullets for identification purposes. The Officer who recovers the bullet must mark his or her initials and the date of recovery of the bullet on the base or on the nose of the bullet.

26. On January 18, 1990, at 11:30 P.M., an unidentified person fired a shot at an unoccupied security patrol car in the facility parking lot. Officer Debra Johnson was assigned to investigate the matter. A fired bullet was recovered inside the patrol car by Officer Johnson at 1:00 A.M. on January 19, 1990.
Officer Johnson should mark *D.J. 1/19/90* on
   A. the base or the nose of the recovered bullet
   B. the side of the recovered bullet
   C. an envelope and place the recovered bullet inside
   D. the side of the patrol car from which the bullet was recovered

Question 27.

DIRECTIONS: Question 27 is to be answered SOLELY on the basis of the following information.

Patrolroom Observers are officers who are assigned to observe events when individuals, other than security staff, are present in the patrolroom. According to facility guidelines, a Patrolroom Observer must be called to the patrolroom to serve as a witness whenever any individual is brought to the patrolroom for any reason by a Special Officer.

27. Janet Childs, a client at Gotham Health Facility, was robbed in the facility's parking lot. Ms. Childs was not harmed as a result of the incident, but she was upset. Special Officer Grey escorted her to the patrolroom, where she remained until she felt better. While she was waiting in the patrolroom, Officer Grey did not call a Patrolman Observer to the patrolroom during the time that Ms. Childs was there.
In this situation, Officer Grey
   A. should not have taken Ms. Childs to the patrolroom without special authorization from his supervisor
   B. was not required to call a Patrolroom Observer to the patrolroom since Ms. Childs had not been placed under arrest
   C. should have called a Patrolroom Observer to be present while Ms. Childs was in the patrolroom
   D. should have escorted Ms. Childs to the patrolroom and left her in the care of the Special Officer assigned to the patrolroom

Question 28.

DIRECTIONS: Question 28 is to be answered SOLELY on the basis of the following information.

Special Officers escort individuals categorized as Emotionally Disturbed Persons to the hospital for observation or treatment when directed to do so. These individuals are transported to the hospital by Emergency Medical Service (EMS) ambulance. There must be one Special Officer present in the ambulance for each Emotionally Disturbed Person transferred to the hospital, along with an EMS Technician and the ambulance driver.

28. Special Officers Patrick Lawson and Grace Martin have   28.____
been assigned to escort two individuals categorized as
Emotionally Disturbed Persons from that facility to a
nearby hospital. The EMS ambulance, with an EMS Technician and ambulance driver, has arrived at the facility
to transport the individuals. Officer Lawson then
suggests to Officer Martin that it is not necessary for
him to go to the hospital since the EMS Technician will
be with Officer Martin in the ambulance.
In this situation, Officer Lawson's suggestion is
- A. *correct*, since an EMS Technician will be present in the ambulance to accompany Officer Martin and the Emotionally Disturbed Persons to the hospital
- B. *incorrect*, since one Special Officer must be present in the ambulance for each Emotionally Disturbed Person transported to the hospital
- C. *correct*, since the Emotionally Disturbed Persons are unlikely to cause any disturbance inside the ambulance
- D. *incorrect*, since two EMS Technicians must be present in the ambulance when only one Special Officer is escorting two Emotionally Disturbed Persons to the hospital

Questions 29-32.

DIRECTIONS: Questions 29 through 32 are to be answered on the basis of the following information.

Assume that information concerning new or updated policies and procedures are sometimes provided to facility security staff in the form of a memorandum from Security Headquarters.

Question 29.

DIRECTIONS: Question 29 is to be answered SOLELY on the basis of the following memorandum.

TO: All Security Officers
FROM: Security Headquarters
SUBJECT: Smoking Regulations

At times, Security Officers have been observed smoking while on duty at their assigned posts. This is strictly prohibited. If Officers feel that they must smoke, they may smoke during breaks or lunch period in designated areas. Officers may not smoke while on official duty. If any Officer is observed smoking while on post or while performing official duties, appropriate disciplinary action will be taken.

29. According to the above memorandum, Security Officers may   29.____
- A. smoke while on duty, as long as they are out of view of the public
- B. not smoke while on duty except when assigned to a post in a designated smoking area

C. smoke on breaks or during lunch period in designated areas
D. not smoke at any time when dressed in official uniform

Question 30.

DIRECTIONS: Question 30 is to be answered SOLELY on the basis of the following memorandum.

TO: All Special Officers
FROM: Security Headquarters
SUBJECT: Safeguarding Shields and Identification Cards

Special Officers must ensure that their shields and identification cards are secure at all times. Should an officer become aware of the loss or theft of his shield or identification card, he shall immediately report such loss or theft to Security Headquarters.

30. According to the above memorandum, a Special Officer must   30.___
    A. report the loss or theft of his identification card to the nearest police precinct
    B. secure his shield in his locker at all times
    C. report the loss or theft of his shield or identification card to Security Headquarters immediately
    D. secure his identification card at Security Headquarters each night before leaving the facility

Question 31.

DIRECTIONS: Question 31 is to be answered SOLELY on the basis of the following memorandum.

TO: All Security Officers
FROM: Security Headquarters
SUBJECT: Fire in the Facility

Special Officers must report immediately to assist at the scene of a fire when directed to do so by a supervisor. Officers shall remain at the scene and ensure that only authorized personnel are in an area restricted by a fire emergency. Visitors and clients shall be directed to the nearest safe stairwell and out of the facility. Visitors and clients are not to use elevators to evacuate the area.

31. According to the above memorandum, a Security Officer   31.___
    should
    A. direct visitors and clients to the nearest elevator in case of fire
    B. report unauthorized personnel at a fire scene to the Fire Department

C. escort visitors and clients down the nearest stairwell and out of the facility
D. ensure that only authorized personnel are in an area restricted by a fire emergency

Question 32.

DIRECTIONS: Question 32 is to be answered SOLELY on the basis of the following memorandum.

TO: All Security Officers
FROM: Security Headquarters
SUBJECT: Reporting Unsafe Conditions

Security Officers shall report to their supervisors and appropriate facility staff any condition that could affect the safety or security of the facility. Conditions such as broken windows, unlocked doors and water leaks should be reported.

32. According to the above memorandum, a Security Officer shall
   A. make recommendations to his superiors concerning other facility staff members
   B. correct all unsafe conditions such as broken windows
   C. report a condition such as a water leak to his supervisor and appropriate facility staff
   D. make recommendations to facility staff concerning doors to be left unlocked

33. Following are two sentences that may or may not be written in correct English:
   I. Special Officer Cleveland was attempting to calm an emotionally disturbed visitor.
   II. The visitor did not stops crying and calling for his wife.
   Which one of the following statements is CORRECT?
   A. Only Sentence I is written in correct English.
   B. Only Sentence II is written in correct English.
   C. Sentences I and II are both written in correct English.
   D. Neither Sentence I nor Sentence II is written in correct English.

34. Following are two sentences that may or may not be written in correct English:
   I. While on patrol, I observes a vagrant loitering near the drug dispensary.
   II. I escorted the vagrant out of the building and off the premises.
   Which one of the following statements is CORRECT?
   A. Only Sentence I is written in correct English.
   B. Only Sentence II is written in correct English.
   C. Sentences I and II are both written in correct English.
   D. Neither Sentence I nor Sentence II is written in correct English.

35. Following are two sentences that may or may not be written in correct English:
   I. At 4:00 P.M., Sergeant Raymond told me to evacuate the waiting area immediately due to a bomb threat.
   II. Some of the clients did not want to leave the building.
   Which one of the following statements is CORRECT?
   A. Only Sentence I is written in correct English.
   B. Only Sentence II is written in correct English.
   C. Sentences I and II are both written in correct English.
   D. Neither Sentence I nor Sentence II is written in correct English.

35.___

KEY (CORRECT ANSWERS)

1. C	11. D	21. D	31. D
2. B	12. C	22. B	32. C
3. A	13. B	23. C	33. A
4. D	14. D	24. A	34. B
5. A	15. C	25. B	35. C
6. B	16. D	26. A	
7. B	17. C	27. C	
8. B	18. D	28. B	
9. B	19. B	29. C	
10. A	20. A	30. C	

MAP READING

EXAMINATION SECTION
TEST 1

DIRECTIONS: Each question or incomplete statement is followed by several suggested answers or completions. Select the one that BEST answers the question or completes the statement. *PRINT THE LETTER OF THE CORRECT ANSWER IN THE SPACE AT THE RIGHT.*

Questions 1-3.

DIRECTIONS: Questions 1 through 3 are to be answered SOLELY on the basis of the map which appears on the next page. The flow of traffic is indicated by the arrow. If there is only one arrow shown, then traffic flows only in the direction indicated by the arrow. If there are two arrows shown, then traffic flows in both directions. You must follow the flow of traffic.

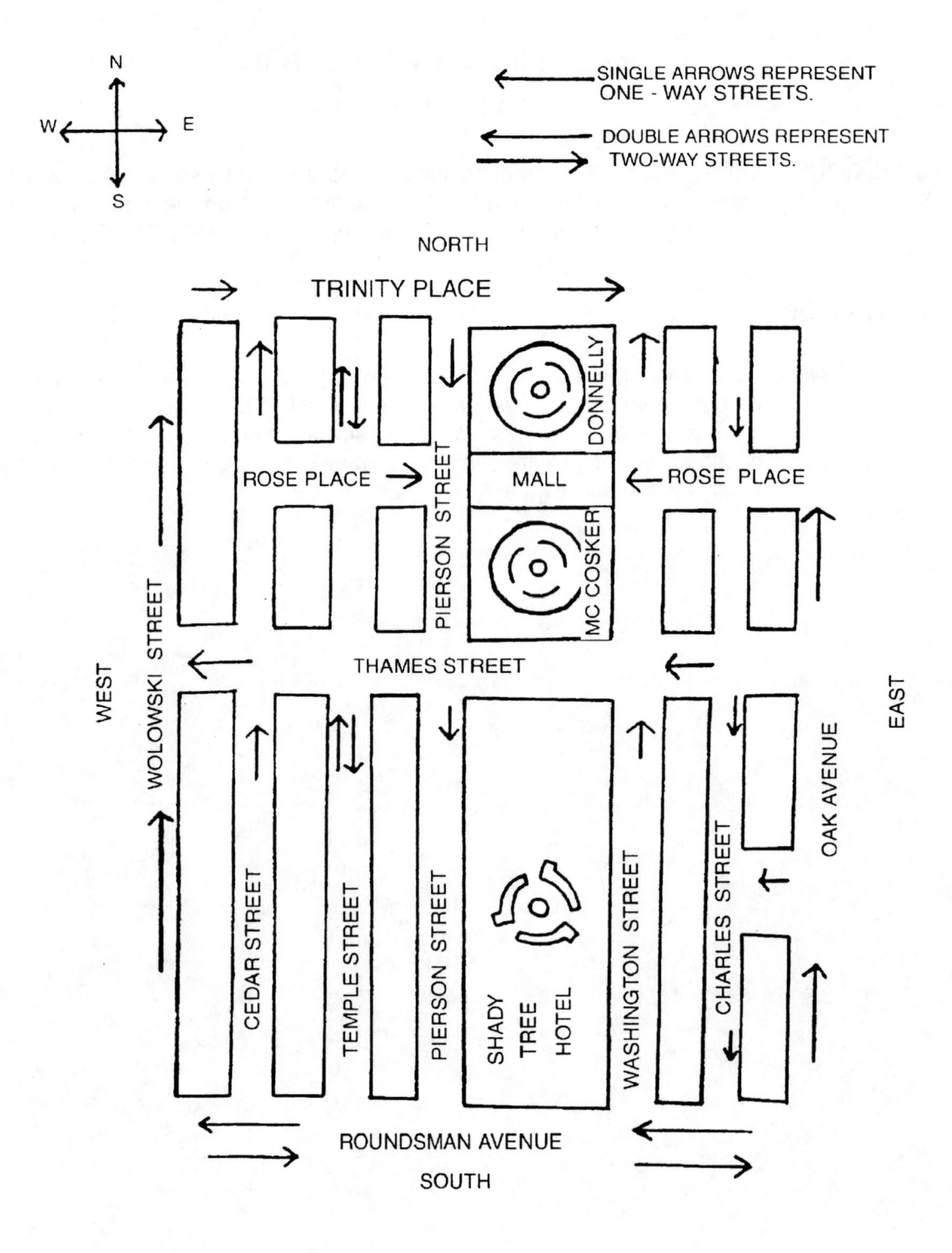

2 (#1)

1. Police Officers Simms and O'Brien are located at Roundsman Avenue and Washington Street. The radio dispatcher has assigned them to investigate a motor vehicle accident at the corner of Pierson Street and Rose Place.
   Which one of the following is the SHORTEST route for them to take in their patrol car, making sure to obey all traffic regulations?
   Travel

   A. west on Roundsman Avenue, then north on Temple Street, then east on Thames Street, then north on Pierson Street to Rose Place
   B. east on Roundsman Avenue, then north on Oak Avenue, then west on Rose Place to Pierson Street
   C. west on Roundsman Avenue, then north on Temple Street, then east on Rose Place to Pierson Street
   D. east on Roundsman Avenue, then north on Oak Avenue, then west on Thames Street, then north on Temple Street, then east on Rose Place to Pierson Street

2. Police Officers Sears and Castro are located at Cedar Street and Roundsman Avenue. They are called to respond to the scene of a burglary at Rose Place and Charles Street. Which one of the following is the SHORTEST route for them to take in their patrol car, making sure to obey all traffic regulations?
   Travel

   A. east on Roundsman Avenue, then north on Oak Avenue, then west on Rose Place to Charles Street
   B. east on Roundsman Avenue, then north on Washington Street, then east on Rose Place to Charles Street
   C. west on Roundsman Avenue, then north on Wolowski Street, then east on Trinity Place, then south on Charles Street to Rose Place
   D. east on Roundsman Avenue, then north on Charles Street to Rose Place

3. Police Officer Glasser is in an unmarked car at the intersection of Rose Place and Temple Street when he begins to follow two robbery suspects. The suspects go south for two blocks, then turn left for two blocks, then make another left turn for one more block. The suspects realize they are being followed and make a left turn and travel two more blocks and then make a right turn.
   In what direction are the suspects now headed?

   A. North   B. South   C. East   D. West

Questions 4-6.

DIRECTIONS: Questions 4 through 6 are to be answered SOLELY on the basis of the following map. The flow of traffic is indicated by the arrows. If there is only one arrow shown, then traffic flows only in the direction indicated by the arrow. If there are two arrows shown, then traffic flows in both directions. You must follow the flow of traffic.

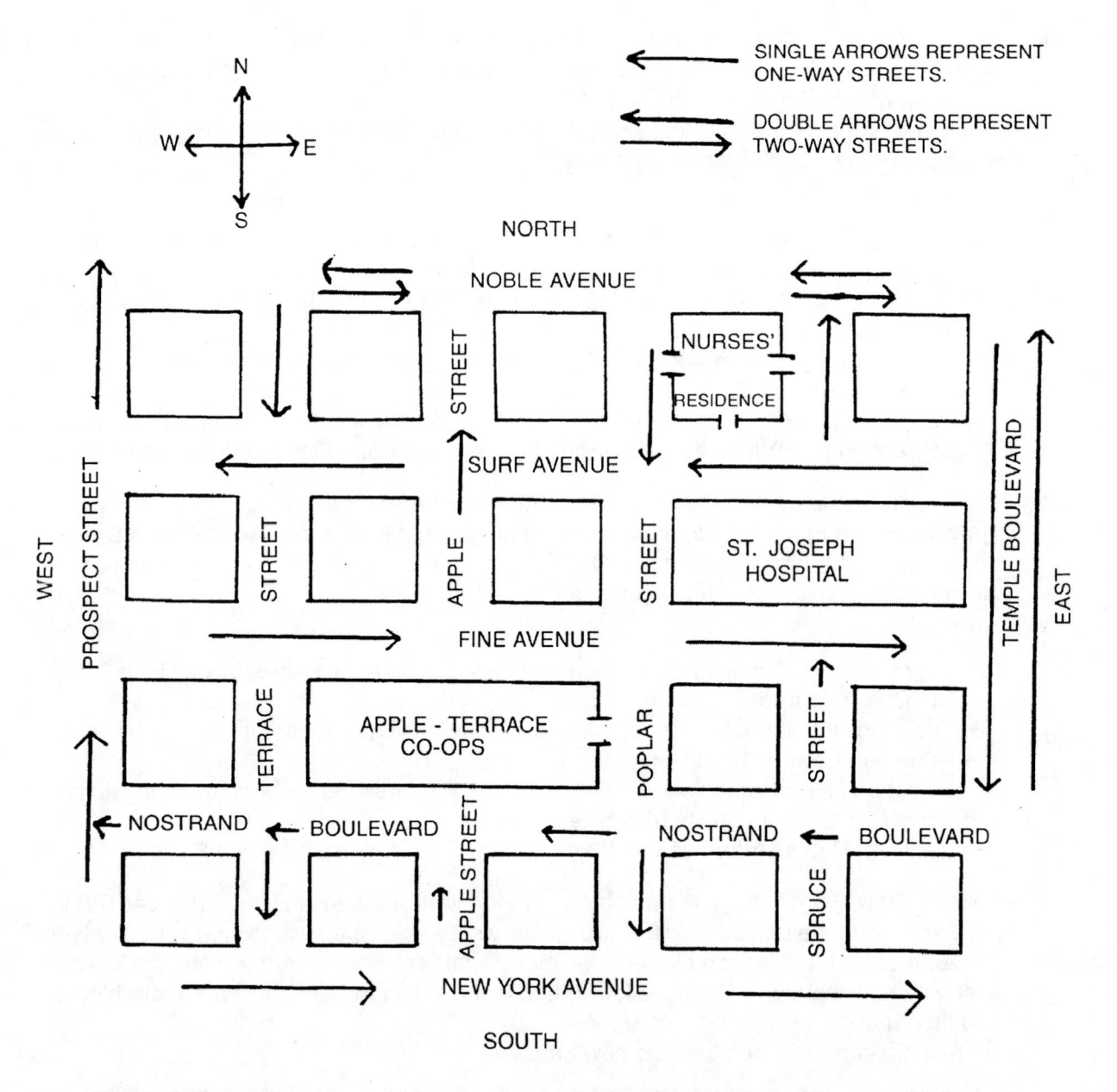

4. Police Officers Gannon and Vine are located at the intersection of Terrace Street and Surf Avenue when they receive a call from the radio dispatcher stating that they need to respond to an attempted murder at Spruce Street and Fine Avenue.
Which one of the following is the SHORTEST route for them to take in their patrol car, making sure to obey all traffic regulations?
Travel _____ to Spruce Street.

- A. west on Surf Avenue, then north on Prospect Street, then east on Noble Avenue, then south on Poplar Street, then east on Fine Avenue
- B. east on Surf Avenue, then south on Poplar Street, then east on Fine Avenue
- C. west on Surf Avenue, then south on Prospect Street, then east on Fine Avenue
- D. south on Terrace Street, then east on Fine Avenue

5. Police Officers Sears and Ronald are at Nostrand Boulevard and Prospect Street. They receive a call assigning them to investigate a disruptive group of youths at Temple Boulevard and Surf Avenue.
Which one of the following is the SHORTEST route for them to take in their patrol car, making sure to obey all traffic regulations?
Travel

   A. north on Prospect Street, then east on Surf Avenue to Temple Boulevard
   B. north on Prospect Street, then east on Noble Avenue, then south on Temple Boulevard to Surf Avenue
   C. north on Prospect Street, then east on Fine Avenue, then north on Temple Boulevard to Surf Avenue
   D. south on Prospect Street, then east on New York Avenue, then north on Temple Boulevard to Surf Avenue

5._____

6. While on patrol at Prospect Street and New York Avenue, Police Officers Ross and Rock are called to a burglary in progress near the entrance to the Apple-Terrace Co-ops on Poplar Street midway between Fine Avenue and Nostrand Boulevard.
Which one of the following is the SHORTEST route for them to take in their patrol car, making sure to obey all traffic regulations?
Travel _____ Poplar Street.

   A. east on New York Avenue, then north
   B. north on Prospect Avenue, then east on Fine Avenue, then south
   C. north on Prospect Street, then east on Surf Avenue, then south
   D. east on New York Avenue, then north on Temple Boulevard, then west on Surf Avenue, then south

6._____

Questions 7-8.

DIRECTIONS: Questions 7 and 8 are to be answered SOLELY on the basis of the map which appears below. The flow of traffic is indicated by the arrows. If there is only one arrow shown, then traffic flows only in the direction indicated by the arrow. If there are two arrows shown, then traffic flows in both directions. You must follow the flow of traffic.

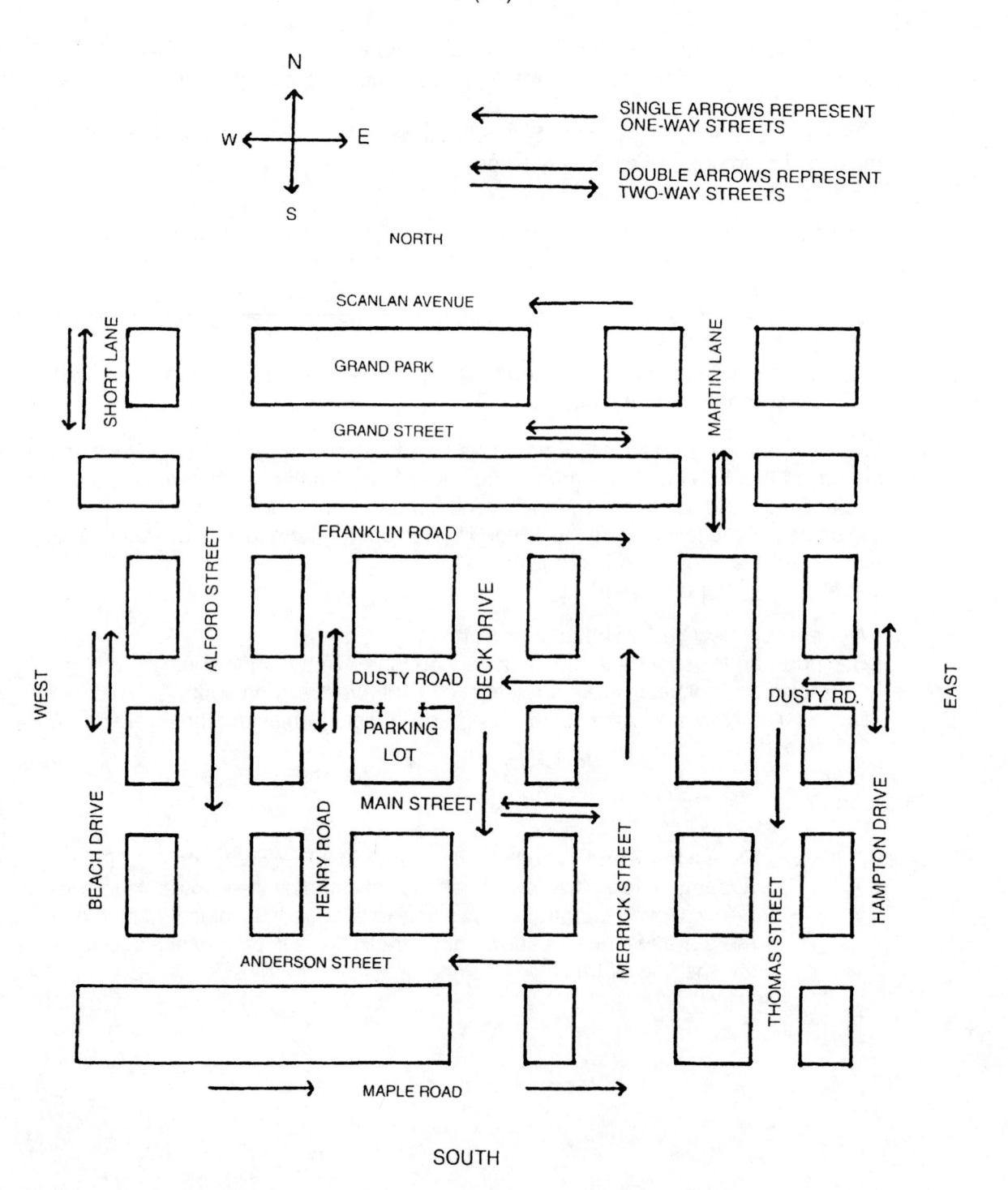

7. Police Officers Gold and Warren are at the intersection of Maple Road and Hampton Drive. The radio dispatcher has assigned them to investigate an attempted auto theft in the parking lot on Dusty Road.
Which one of the following is the SHORTEST route for the officers to take in their patrol car to get to the entrance of the parking lot on Dusty Road, making sure to obey all traffic regulations?
Travel _____ to the parking lot entrance.

A. north on Hampton Drive, then west on Dusty Road
B. west on Maple Road, then north on Beck Drive, then west on Dusty Road
C. north on Hampton Drive, then west on Anderson Street, then north on Merrick Street, then west on Dusty Road
D. west on Maple Road, then north on Merrick Street, then west on Dusty Road

8. Police Officer Gladden is in a patrol car at the intersection of Beach Drive and Anderson Street when he spots a suspicious car. Police Officer Gladden calls the radio dispatcher to determine if the vehicle was stolen. Police Officer Gladden then follows the vehicle north on Beach Drive for three blocks, then turns right and proceeds for one block and makes another right. He then follows the vehicle for two blocks, and then they both make a left turn and continue driving. Police Officer Gladden now receives a call from the dispatcher stating the car was reported stolen and signals for the vehicle to pull to the side of the road.
In what direction was Police Officer Gladden heading at the time he signaled for the other car to pull over?

   A. North   B. East   C. South   D. West

8._____

Questions 9-10.

DIRECTIONS: Questions 9 and 10 are to be answered SOLELY on the basis of the map which appears on the following page. The flow of traffic is indicated by the arrows. If there is only one arrow shown, then traffic flows only in the direction indicated by the arrow. If there are two arrows shown, then traffic flows in both directions. You must follow the flow of traffic.

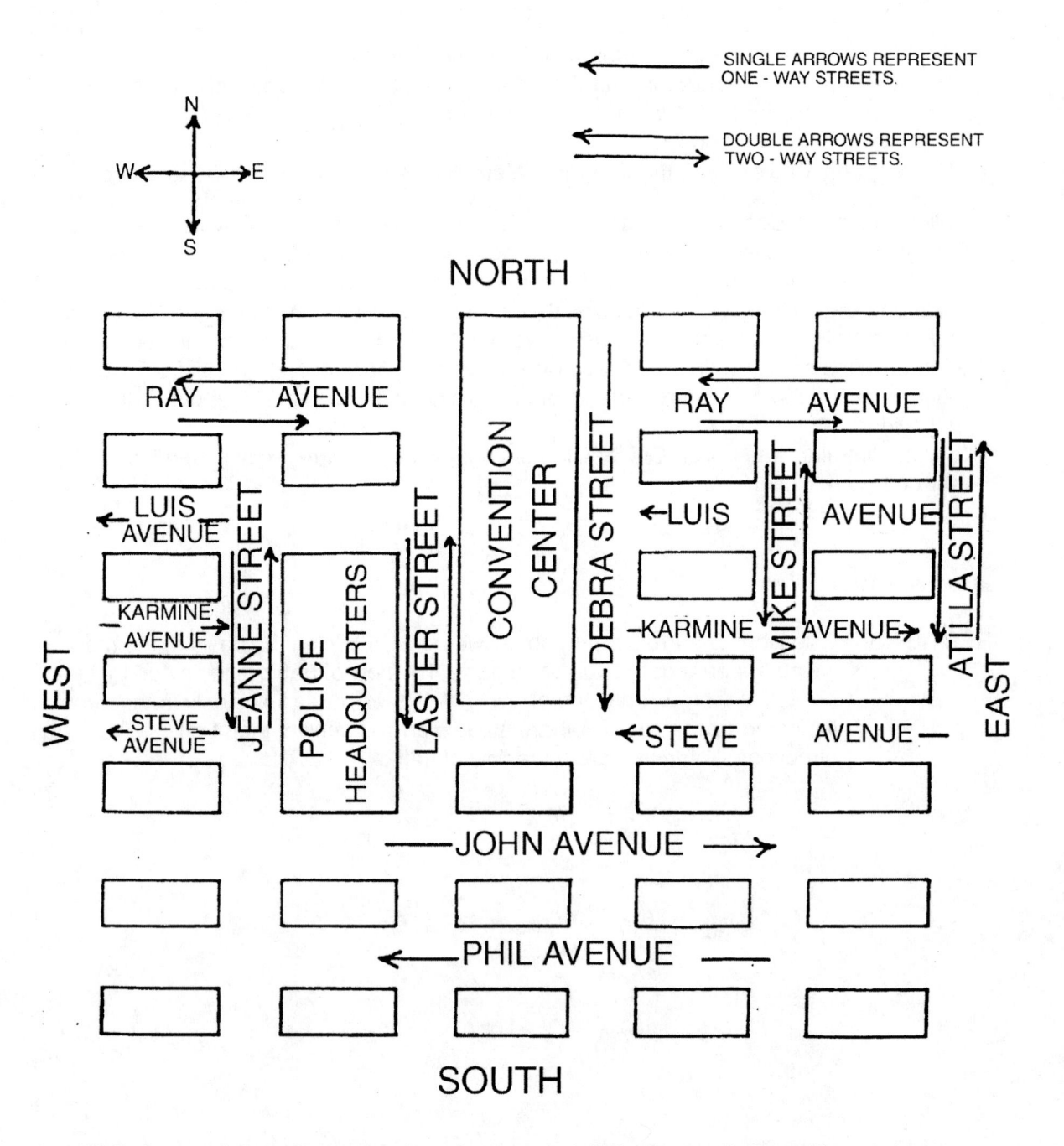

9. While in a patrol car located at Ray Avenue and Atilla Street, Police Officer Ashley receives a call from the dispatcher to respond to an assault at Jeanne Street and Karmine Avenue.
Which one of the following is the SHORTEST route for Officer Ashley to follow in his patrol car, making sure to obey all traffic regulations?
Travel

   A. south on Atilla Street, west on Luis Avenue, south on Debra Street, west on Steve Avenue, north on Lester Street, west on Luis Avenue, then one block south on Jeanne Street
   B. south on Atilla Street, then four blocks west on Phil Avenue, then north on Jeanne Street to Karmine Avenue

C. west on Ray Avenue to Debra Street, then five blocks south to Phil Avenue, then west to Jeanne Street, then three blocks north to Karmine Avenue
D. south on Atilla Street, then four blocks west on John Avenue, then north on Jeanne Street to Karmine Avenue

10. After taking a complaint report from the assault victim, Officer Ashley receives a call from the dispatcher to respond to an auto larceny in progress at the corner of Debra Street and Luis Avenue.
Which one of the following is the SHORTEST route for Officer Ashley to follow in his patrol car, making sure to obey all traffic regulations?
Travel

A. south on Jeanne Street to John Avenue, then east three blocks on John Avenue, then north on Mike Street to Luis Avenue, then west to Debra Street
B. south on Jeanne Street to John Avenue, then east two blocks on John Avenue, then north on Debra Street to Luis Avenue
C. north on Jeanne Street two blocks, then east on Ray Avenue for one block, then south on Lester Street to Steve Avenue, then one block east on Steve Avenue, then north on Debra Street to Luis Avenue
D. south on Jeanne Street to John Avenue, then east on John Avenue to Atilla Street, then north three blocks to Luis Avenue, then west to Debra Street

Questions 11-13.

DIRECTIONS: Questions 11 through 13 are to be answered SOLELY on the basis of the following map. The flow of traffic is indicated by the arrows. You must follow the flow of traffic.

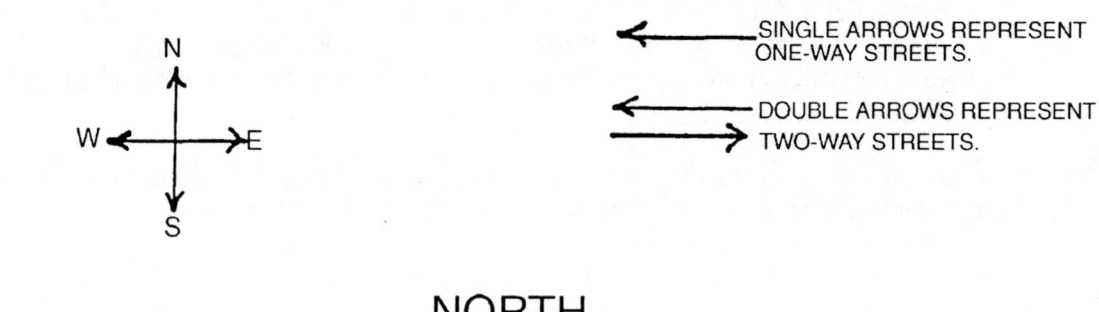

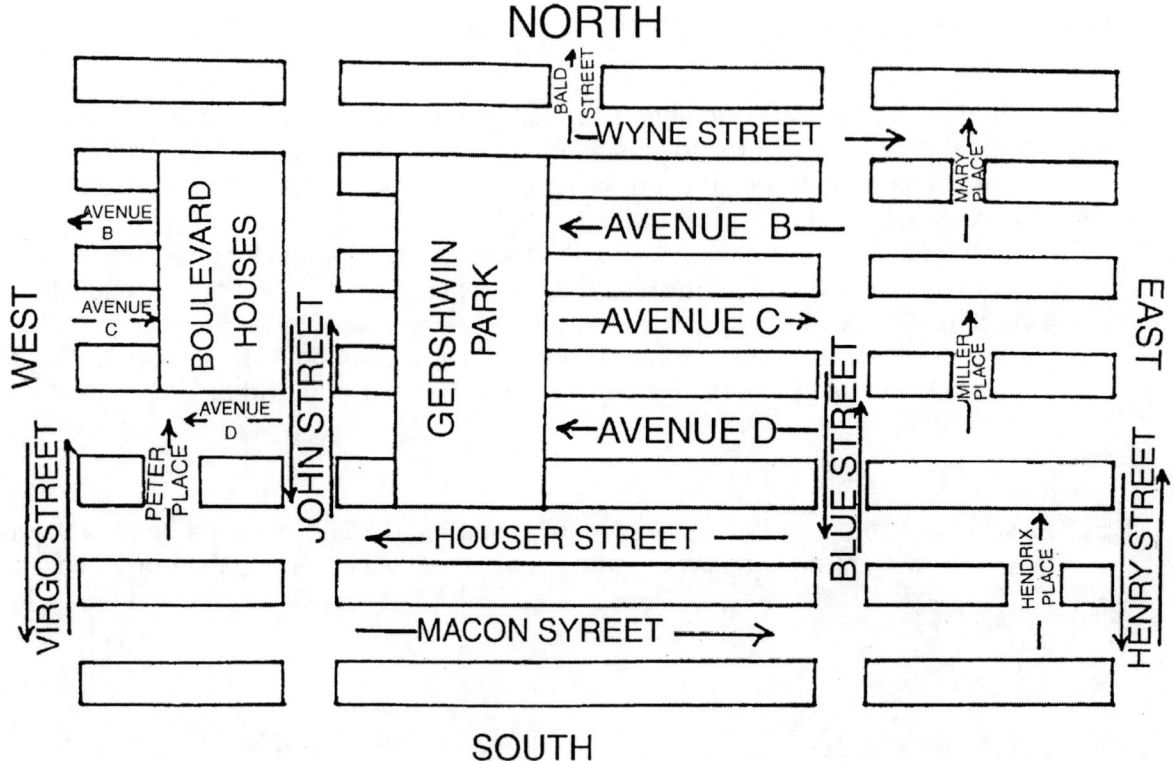

11. Police Officers Ranking and Fish are located at Wyne Street and John Street. The radio dispatcher has assigned them to investigate a motor vehicle accident at the corner of Henry Street and Houser Street.
Which one of the following is the SHORTEST route for them to take in their patrol car, making sure to obey all traffic regulations?
Travel

   A. four blocks south on John Street, then three blocks east on Houser Street to Henry Street
   B. two blocks east on Wyne Street, then two blocks south on Blue Street, then two blocks east on Avenue C, then two blocks south on Henry Street
   C. two blocks east on Wyne Street, then five blocks south on Blue Street, then two blocks east on Macon Street, then one block north on Henry Street
   D. five blocks south on John Street, then three blocks east on Macon Street, then one block north to Houser Street

12. Police Officers Rizzo and Latimer are located at Avenue B and Virgo Street. They respond to the scene of a robbery at Miller Place and Avenue D.
Which one of the following is the SHORTEST route for them to take in their patrol car, making sure to obey all traffic regulations?
Travel _____ to Miller Place.

   A. one block north on Virgo Street, then four blocks east on Wyne Street, then three blocks south on Henry Street, then one block west on Avenue D
   B. four blocks south on Virgo Street, then two blocks east on Macon Street, then two blocks north on Blue Street, then one block east on Avenue D
   C. three blocks south on Virgo Street, then east on Houser Street to Henry Street, then one block north on Henry Street, then one block west on Avenue D
   D. four blocks south on Virgo Street, then four blocks east to Henry Street, then north to Avenue D, then one block west

13. Police Officer Bendix is in an unmarked patrol car at the intersection of John Street and Macon Street when he begins to follow a robbery suspect. The suspect goes one block east, turns left, travels for three blocks, and then turns right. He drives for two blocks and then makes a right turn. In the middle of the block, the suspect realizes he is being followed and makes a u-turn. In what direction is the suspect now headed?

   A. North   B. South   C. East   D. West

Questions 14-15.

DIRECTIONS: Questions 14 and 15 are to be answered SOLELY on the basis of the following map. The flow of traffic is indicated by the arrows. If there is only one arrow shown, then traffic flows only in the direction indicated by the arrow. If there are two arrows shown, then traffic flows in both directions. You must follow the flow of traffic.

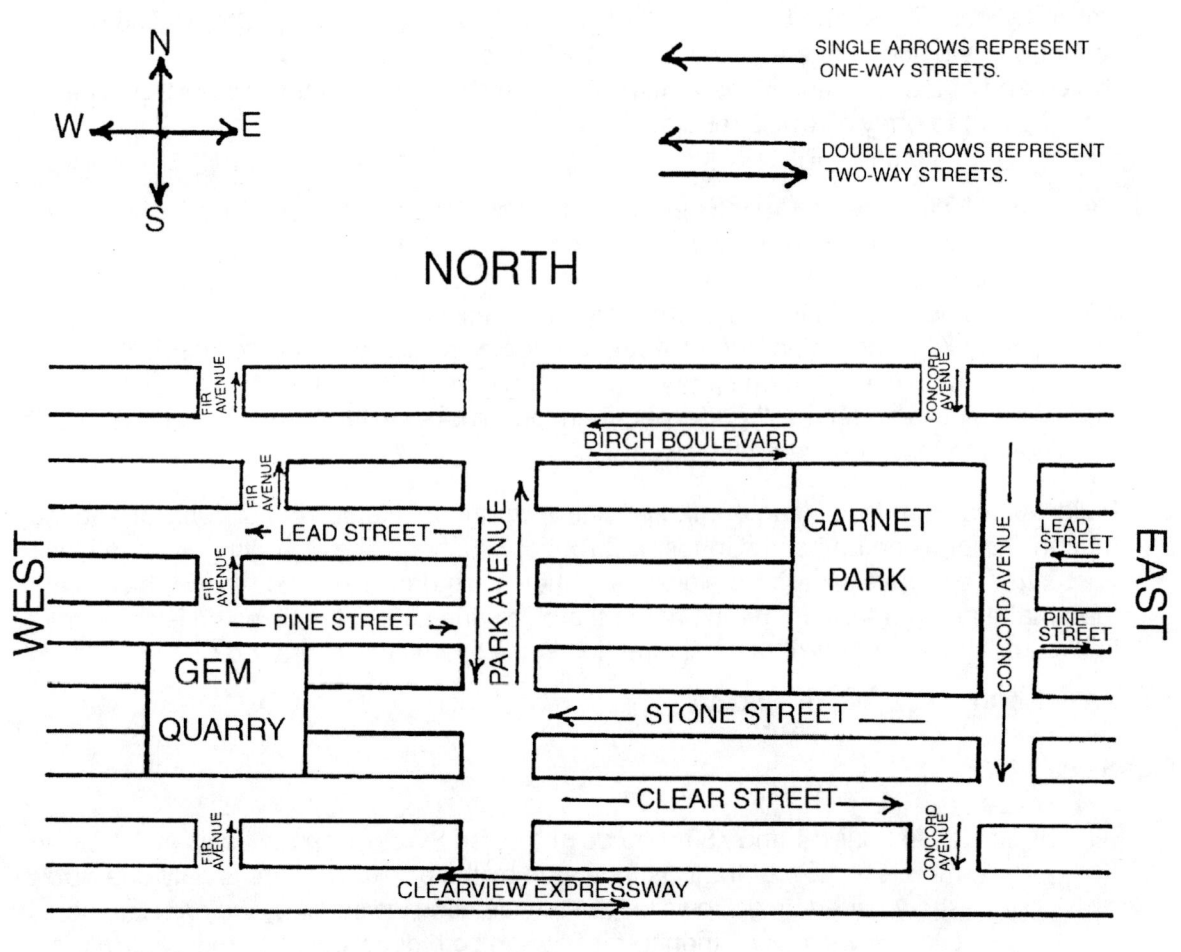

14. You are located at Fir Avenue and Birch Boulevard and receive a request to respond to a disturbance at Fir Avenue and Clear Street.
Which one of the following is the MOST direct route for you to take in your patrol car, making sure to obey all traffic regulations?
Travel

   A. one block east on Birch Boulevard, then four blocks south on Park Avenue, then one block east on Clear Street
   B. two blocks east on Birch Boulevard, then three blocks south on Concord Avenue, then two blocks west on Stone Street, then one block south on Park Avenue, then one block west on Clear Street
   C. one block east on Birch Boulevard, then five blocks south on Park Avenue, then one block west on the Clearview Expressway, then one block north on Fir Avenue
   D. two blocks south on Fir Avenue, then one block east on Pine Street, then three blocks south on Park Avenue, then one block east on the Clearview Expressway, then one block north on Fir Avenue

15. You are located at the Clearview Expressway and Concord Avenue and receive a call to respond to a crime in progress at Concord Avenue and Pine Street. Which one of the following is the MOST direct route for you to take in your patrol car, making sure to obey all traffic regulations?
Travel

    A. two blocks west on the Clearview Expressway, then one block north on Fir Avenue, then one block east on Clear Street, then four blocks north on Park Avenue, then one block east on Birch Boulevard, then two blocks south on Concord Avenue
    B. one block north on Concord Avenue, then one block west on Clear Street, then one block north on Park Avenue, then one block east on Stone Street, then one block north on Concord Avenue
    C. one block west on the Clearview Expressway, then four blocks north on Park Avenue, then one block west on Lead Street, then one block south on Fir Avenue
    D. one block west on the Clearview Expressway, then five blocks north on Park Avenue, then one block east on Birch Boulevard, then two blocks south on Concord Avenue

15.____

Questions 16-20.

DIRECTIONS: Questions 16 through 20 are to be answered SOLELY on the basis of the following map. The flow of traffic is indicated by the arrows. You must follow the flow of traffic.

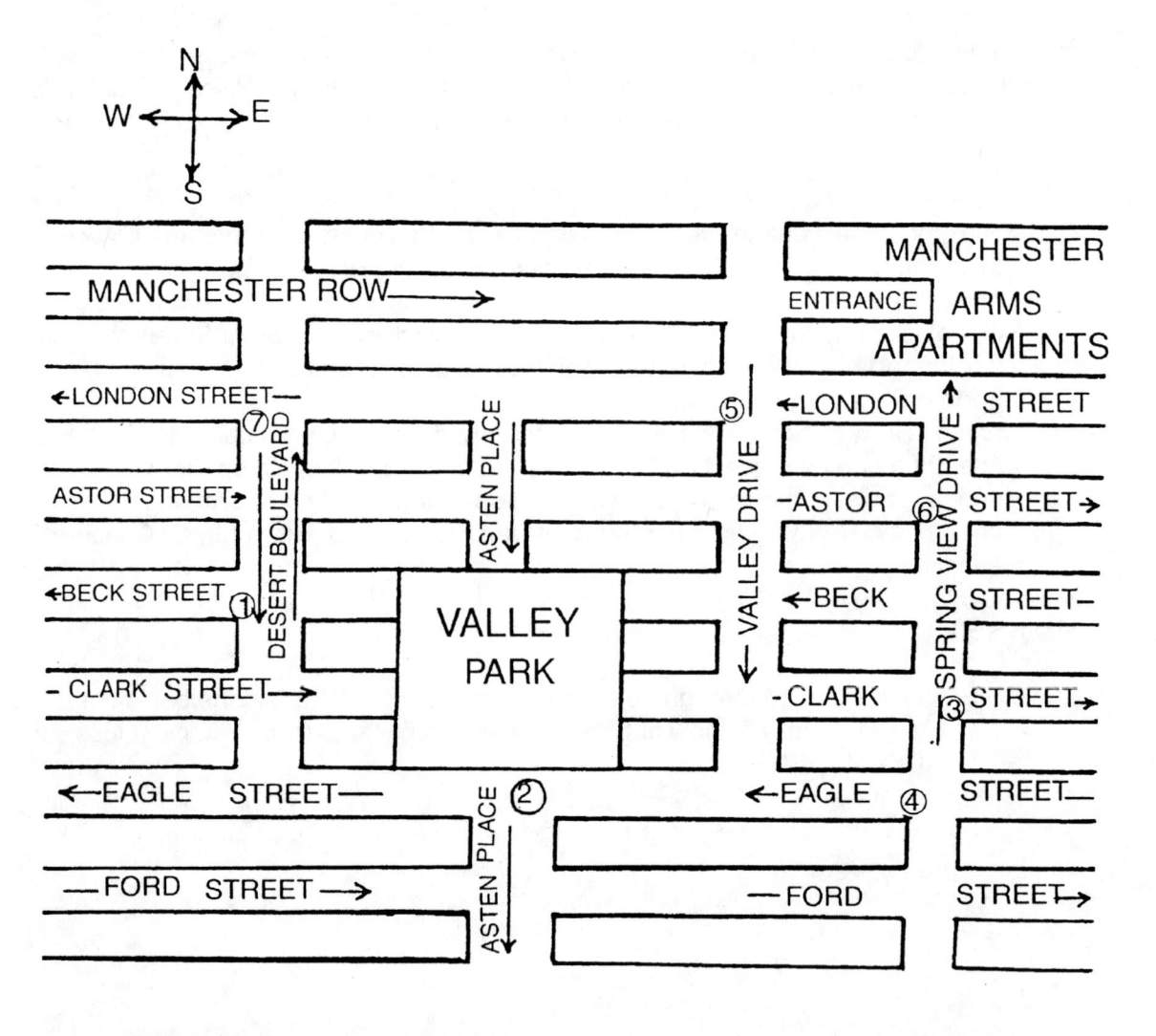

16. If you are located at Point 7 and travel south for one block, then turn east and travel two blocks, then turn south and travel two blocks, then turn east and travel one block, you will be CLOSEST to Point

    A. 2   B. 3   C. 4   D. 6

17. If you are located at Point 3 and travel north for one block, and then turn west and travel one block, and then turn south and travel two blocks, and then turn west and travel one block, you will be CLOSEST to Point

    A. 1   B. 2   C. 4   D. 6

18. You are located at Astor Street and Spring View Drive. You receive a call of a crime in progress at the intersection of Beck Street and Desert Boulevard.
    Which one of the following is the MOST direct route for you to take in your patrol car, making sure to obey all traffic regulations?
    Travel

    A. one block north on Spring View Drive, then three blocks west on London Street, then two blocks south on Desert Boulevard
    B. three blocks west on Astor Street, then one block south on Desert Boulevard

C. one block south on Spring View Drive, then three blocks west on Beck Street
D. three blocks south on Spring View Drive, then three blocks west on Eagle Street, then two blocks north on Desert Boulevard

19. You are located on Clark Street and Desert Boulevard and must respond to a disturbance at Clark Street and Spring View Drive.
Which one of the following is the MOST direct route for you to take in your patrol car, making sure to obey all traffic regulations?
Travel

   A. two blocks north on Desert Boulevard, then three blocks east on Astor Street, then two blocks south on Spring View Drive
   B. one block south on Desert Boulevard, then three blocks east on Eagle Street, then one block north on Spring View Drive
   C. two blocks north on Desert Boulevard, then two blocks east on Astor Street, then three blocks south on Valley Drive, then one block east on Eagle Street, then one block north on Spring View Drive
   D. two blocks north on Desert Boulevard, then two blocks east on Astor Street, then two blocks south on Valley Drive, then one block east on Clark Street

19.____

20. You are located at Valley Drive and Beck Street and receive a call to respond to the corner of Asten Place and Astor Street.
Which one of the following is the MOST direct route for you to take in your patrol car, making sure to obey all traffic regulations?
Travel _____ on Astor Street.

   A. one block north on Valley Drive, then one block west
   B. two blocks south on Valley Drive, then one block east on Eagle Street, then three blocks north on Spring View Drive, then two blocks west
   C. two blocks south on Valley Drive, then two blocks west on Eagle Street, then three blocks north on Desert Boulevard, then one block east
   D. one block south on Valley Drive, then one block east on Clark Street, then two blocks north on Spring View Drive, then two blocks west

20.____

KEY (CORRECT ANSWERS)

1.	C	11.	B
2.	A	12.	A
3.	A	13.	A
4.	D	14.	C
5.	C	15.	D
6.	B	16.	B
7.	C	17.	B
8.	B	18.	A
9.	A	19.	D
10.	A	20.	C

READING COMPREHENSION
UNDERSTANDING, AND INTERPRETING WRITTEN MATERIAL
COMMENTARY

The ability to read, understand, and interpret written materials - texts, publications, newspapers, orders, directions, expositions, legal passages - is a skill basic to a functioning democracy and to an efficient business or viable government.

That is why almost all examinations - for beginning, middle, and senior levels - test reading comprehension, directly or indirectly.

The reading test measures how well you understand what you read. This is how it is done: You read a paragraph and several statements based on a question. From the statements, you choose the *one* statement, or answer, that is *BEST* supported by, or *BEST* matches, what is said in the paragraph.

SAMPLE QUESTIONS

DIRECTIONS: Each question has five suggested answers, lettered A, B, C, D, and E. Decide which one is the *BEST* answer. *PRINT THE LETTER OF THE CORRECT ANSWER IN THE SPACE AT THE RIGHT.*

1. The prevention of accidents makes it necessary not only that safety devices be used to guard exposed machinery but also that mechanics be instructed in safety rules which they must follow for their own protection and that the light in the plant be adequate.
   The paragraph BEST supports the statement that industrial accidents
   A. are always avoidable
   B. may be due to ignorance
   C. usually result from inadequate machinery
   D. cannot be entirely overcome
   E. result in damage to machinery

ANALYSIS

Remember what you have to do -
   First - Read the paragraph.
   Second - Decide what the paragraph means.
   Third - Read the five suggested answers.
   Fourth - Select the one answer which *BEST* matches what the paragraph says or is *BEST* supported by something in the paragraph. (Sometimes you may have to read the paragraph again in order to be sure which suggested answer is best.)

This paragraph is talking about three steps that should be taken to prevent industrial accidents -
   1. use safety devices on machines
   2. instruct mechanics in safety rules
   3. provide adequate lighting.

SELECTION

With this in mind, let's look at each suggested answer. Each one starts with "Industrial accidents ..."

SUGGESTED ANSWER A.
   Industrial accidents (A) are always avoidable.
   (The paragraph talks about how to avoid accidents but does not say that accidents are always avoidable.)

SUGGESTED ANSWER B.
   Industrial accidents (B) may be due to ignorance.
   (One of the steps given in the paragraph to prevent accidents is to instruct mechanics on safety rules. This suggests that lack of knowledge or ignorance of safety rules causes accidents. This suggested answer sounds like a good possibility for being the right answer.)
SUGGESTED ANSWER C.
   Industrial accidents (C) usually result from inadequate machinery.
   (The paragraph does suggest that exposed machines cause accidents, but it doesn't say that it is the usual cause of accidents. The word *usually* makes this a wrong answer.)
SUGGESTED ANSWER D.
   Industrial accidents (D) cannot be entirely overcome.
   (You may know from your own experience that this is a true statement. But that is not what the paragraph is talking about. Therefore, it is NOT the correct answer.)
SUGGESTED ANSWER E.
   Industrial accidents (E) result in damage to machinery.
   (This is a statement that may or may not be true, but, in any case, it is NOT covered by the paragraph.)

Looking back, you see that the one suggested answer of the five given that *BEST* matches what the paragraph says is -
   Industrial accidents (B) may be due to ignorance.
   The *CORRECT* answer then is B.
   Be sure you read *ALL* the possible answers before you make your choice. You may think that none of the five answers is really good, but choose the *BEST* one of the five.

---

2. Probably few people realize, as they drive on a concrete road, that steel is used to keep the surface flat in spite of the weight of the busses and trucks. Steel bars, deeply embedded in the concrete, provide sinews to take the stresses so that the stresses cannot crack the slab or make it wavy.
   The paragraph BEST supports the statement THAT a concrete road
      A. is expensive to build
      B. usually cracks under heavy weights
      C. looks like any other road
      D. is used only for heavy traffic
      E. is reinforced with other material

ANALYSIS
This paragraph is commenting on the fact that -
   1. few people realize, as they drive on a concrete road, that steel is deeply embedded
   2. steel keeps the surface flat
   3. steel bars enable the road to take the stresses without cracking or becoming wavy.

SELECTION
Now read and think about the possible answers:
   A. A concrete road is expensive to build.
      (Maybe so but that is not what the paragraph is about.)

B. A concrete road usually cracks under heavy weights.
   (The paragraph talks about using steel bars to prevent heavy weights from cracking concrete roads. It says nothing about how usual it is for the roads to crack. The word *usually* makes this suggested answer wrong.)
C. A concrete road looks like any other road.
   (This may or may not be true. The important thing to note is that it has nothing to do with what the paragraph is about.)
D. A concrete road is used only for heavy traffic.
   (This answer at least has something to do with the paragraph - concrete roads are used with heavy traffic but it does not say "used only.")
E. A concrete road is reinforced with other material.
   (This choice seems to be the correct one on two counts: *First*, the paragraph does suggest that concrete roads are made stronger by embedding steel bars in them. This is another way of saying "concrete roads are reinforced with steel bars." *Second*, by the process of elimination, the other four choices are ruled out as correct answers simply because they do not apply.)

You can be sure that not all the reading questions will be so easy as these.

SUGGESTIONS FOR ANSWERING READING QUESTIONS

1. Read the paragraph carefully. Then read each suggested answer carefully. Read every word, because often one word can make the difference between a right and a wrong answer.
2. Choose that answer which is supported in the paragraph itself. Do not choose an answer which is a correct statement unless it is based on information in the paragraph.
3. Even though a suggested answer has many of the words used in the paragraph, it may still be wrong.
4. Look out for words - such as *always, never, entirely, or only* - which tend to make a suggested answer wrong.
5. Answer first those questions which you can answer most easily. Then work on the other questions.
6. If you can't figure out the answer to the question, guess.

EXAMINATION SECTION

DIRECTIONS FOR THIS SECTION:
   The following questions are intended to test your ability to read with comprehension and to understand and interpret written materials, particularly legal passages.
   Each question has several suggested answers. *PRINT THE LETTER OF THE CORRECT ANSWER IN THE SPACE AT THE RIGHT.*
   It will be necessary for you to read each paragraph carefully because the questions are based only on the material contained therein.

TEST 1

Questions 1-3.
DIRECTIONS: Answer Questions 1 to 3 *SOLELY* on the basis of the following situation:
   When police officers search for a stolen car, they first check for the color of the car, then for make, model, year, body damage and,

finally, license number. The first five can be detected from almost any angle, while the recognition of the license number is often not immediately apparent. The serial number and motor number, though less likely to be changed than the easily substituted license number, cannot be observed in initial detection of the stolen car.

1. According to the above paragraph, the *one* of the following features which is *LEAST* readily observed in checking for a stolen car in moving traffic is:
    A. License number B. Serial number C. Model
    D. Make   E. Color

2. The feature of a car that *CANNOT* be determined from most angles of observation is the
    A. make   B. model   C. year
    D. license number E. color

3. Of the following, the feature of a stolen car that is *MOST* likely to be altered by a car thief shortly after the car is stolen is the
    A. license number B. motor number   C. color
    D. model   E. minor body damage

Questions 4-5.
DIRECTIONS: Answer Questions 4 and 5 *SOLELY* on the basis of the following statement:

The racketeer is primarily concerned with business affairs, legitimate or otherwise, and preferably those which are close to the margin of legitimacy. He gets his best opportunities from business organizations which meet the need of large sections of the public for goods or services which are defined as illegitimate by the same public, such as prostitution, gambling, illicit drugs or liquor. In contrast to the thief, the racketeer and the establishments he controls deliver goods and services for money received.

4. From the above paragraph, it can be *deduced* that suppression of racketeers is *DIFFICULT* because
    A. victims of racketeers are not guilty of violating the law
    B. racketeers are generally engaged in fully legitimate enterprises
    C. many people want services which are not obtainable through legitimate sources
    D. the racketeers are well organized
    E. laws prohibiting gambling and prostitution are unenforceable

5. According to the above paragraph, racketeering, unlike theft, involves
    A. objects of value   B. payment for goods received
    C. organized gangs   D. public approval
    E. unlawful activities

Questions 6-8.
DIRECTIONS: Answer Questions 6 to 8 *SOLELY* on the basis of the following statement:

A number of crimes, such as robbery, assault, rape, certain forms of theft and burglary, are high visibility crimes in that it is apparent to all concerned that they are criminal acts prior to or at the time they are committed. In contrast to these, check forgeries, especially those committed by first offenders, have low visibility. There is little in the criminal act or in the interaction between the check passer and the person cashing the check to identify it as a crime. Closely related to this special quality of the forgery crime is the fact that, while it is formally defined and treated as a felonious or "infamous" crime, it is informally held by the legally untrained public to be a relatively harmless form of crime.

6. According to the above paragraph, crimes of "high visibility"   6. ...
   A. are immediately recognized as crimes by the victims
   B. take place in public view
   C. always involve violence or the threat of violence
   D. usually are committed after dark
   E. can be observed from a distance

7. According to the above paragraph,   7. ...
   A. the public regards check forgery as a minor crime
   B. the law regards check forgery as a minor crime
   C. the law distinguishes between check forgery and other forgery
   D. it is easier to spot inexperienced check forgers than other criminals
   E. it is more difficult to identify check forgers than other criminals

8. As used in this paragraph, an "infamous" crime is   8. ...
   A. a crime attracting great attention from the public
   B. more serious than a felony
   C. less serious than a felony
   D. more or less serious than a felony, depending upon the surrounding circumstances
   E. the same as a felony

Questions 9-11.
DIRECTIONS: Answer Questions 9 to 11 *SOLELY* on the basis of the following statement:
   Criminal science is largely the science of identification. Progress in this field has been marked and sometimes very spectacular because new techniques, instruments and facts flow continuously from the scientists. But the crime laboratories are undermanned, trade secrets still prevail, and inaccurate conclusions are often the result. However, modern gadgets cannot substitute for the skilled intelligent investigator; he must be their master.

9. According to this paragraph, criminal science   9. ...
   A. excludes the field of investigation
   B. is primarily interested in establishing identity
   C. is based on the equipment used in crime laboratories
   D. uses techniques different from those used in other sciences
   E. is essentially secret in nature

10. Advances in criminal science have been, according to the above paragraph,   10. ...
    A. extremely limited   B. slow but steady
    C. unusually reliable   D. outstanding
    E. infrequently worthwhile

11. A problem that has *NOT* been overcome *completely* in crime work is, according to the above paragraph,   11. ...
    A. unskilled investigators
    B. the expense of new equipment and techniques
    C. an insufficient number of personnel in crime laboratories
    D. inaccurate equipment used in laboratories
    E. conclusions of the public about the value of this field

Test 1

Questions 12-14.
DIRECTIONS: Answer Questions 12 to 14 *SOLELY* on the basis of the following statement:

The New York City Police Department will accept for investigation no report of a person missing from his residence if such residence is located outside of New York City. The person reporting same will be advised to report such fact to the police department of the locality where the missing person lives, which will, if necessary, communicate officially with the New York City Police Department. However, a report will be accepted of a person who is missing from a temporary residence in New York City, but the person making the report will be instructed to make a report also to the police department of the locality where the missing person lives.

12. According to the above paragraph, a report to the New York City Police Department of a missing person whose permanent residence is outside of New York City will   12. ...
    A. *always be* investigated provided that a report is also made to his local police authorities
    B. *never be* investigated unless requested officially by his local police authorities
    C. *be* investigated in cases of temporary New York City residence, but a report should always be made to his local police authorities
    D. *be* investigated if the person making the report is a New York City resident
    E. *always be* investigated and a report will be made to the local police authorities by the New York City Police Department

13. Of the following, the *most likely* reason for the procedure described in the above paragraph is that   13. ...
    A. non-residents are not entitled to free police services from New York City
    B. local police authorities would resent interference in their jurisdiction
    C. local police authorities sometimes try to unload their problems on the New York City police
    D. local police authorities may be better able to conduct an investigation
    E. few persons are erroneously reported as missing

14. Mr. Smith, who lives in Jersey City, and Mr. Jones, who lives in Newark, arrange to meet in New York City, but Mr. Jones doesn't keep the appointment. Mr. Smith telephones Mr. Jones several times the next day and gets no answer. Mr. Smith believes that something has happened to Mr. Jones. According to the above paragraph, Mr. Smith should apply to the police authorities of   14. ...
    A. Jersey City   B. Newark
    C. Newark and New York City   D. Jersey City and New York City
    E. Newark, Jersey City, and New York City

Questions 15-17.
DIRECTIONS: Answer Questions 15 to 17 *SOLELY* on the basis of the following statement:

Some early psychologists believed that the basic characteristic of the criminal type was inferiority of intelligence, if not outright feeble-mindedness. They were misled by the fact that they had measurements for all kinds of criminals but, until World War I gave them a draft-army sample, they had no information on a comparable group of non-criminal adults. As soon as acceptable measurements could be taken of criminals and a comparable group of non-criminals, concern with feeblemindedness or with low intelligence as a type took on less and less significance in research in criminology.

15. According to the above paragraph, some early psychologists were in error because they *didn't* 15. ...
    A. distinguish among the various types of criminals
    B. devise a suitable method of measuring intelligence
    C. measure the intelligence of non-criminals as a basis for comparison
    D. distinguish between feeblemindedness and inferiority of intelligence
    E. clearly define the term "intelligence"

16. The above paragraph *implies* that studies of the intelligence of criminals and non-criminals 16. ...
    A. are useless because it is impossible to obtain comparable groups
    B. are not meaningful because only the less intelligent criminals are detected
    C. indicate that criminals are more intelligent than non-criminals
    D. indicate that criminals are less intelligent than non-criminals
    E. do not indicate that there are any differences between the two groups

17. According to the above paragraph, studies of the World War I draft gave psychologists vital information concerning 17. ...
    A. adaptability to army life of criminals and non-criminals
    B. criminal tendencies among draftees
    C. the intelligence scores of large numbers of men
    D. differences between intelligence scores of draftees and volunteers
    E. the behavior of men under abnormal conditions

Questions 18-20.
DIRECTIONS: Answer Questions 18 to 20 *SOLELY* on the basis of the following statement:

The use of a roadblock is simply an adaptation to police practice of the military concept of encirclement. Successful operation of a roadblock plan depends almost entirely on the amount of advance study and planning given to such operations. A thorough and detailed examination of the roads and terrain under the jurisdiction of a given police agency should be made with the locations of the roadblocks pinpointed in advance. The first principle to be borne in mind in the location of each roadblock is the time element. Its location must be at a point beyond which the fugitive could not have possibly traveled in the time elapsed from the commission of the crime to the arrival of the officers at the roadblock.

18. According to the above paragraph, 18. ...
    A. military operations have made extensive use of roadblocks
    B. the military concept of encirclement is an adaptation of police use of roadblocks
    C. the technique of encirclement has been widely used by military forces

    D. a roadblock is generally more effective than encirclement
    E. police use of roadblocks is based on the idea of military encirclement
19. According to the above paragraph,
    A. the factor of time is the sole consideration in the location of a roadblock
    B. the maximum speed possible in the method of escape is of major importance in roadblock location
    C. the time of arrival of officers at the site of a proposed roadblock is of little importance
    D. if the method of escape is not known it should be assumed that the escape is by automobile
    E. a roadblock should be sited as close to the scene of the crime as the terrain will permit
20. According to the above paragraph,
    A. advance study and planning are of minor importance in the success of roadblock operations
    B. a thorough and detailed examination of all roads within a radius of fifty miles should precede the determination of a roadblock location
    C. consideration of terrain features are important in planning the location of roadblocks
    D. the pinpointing of roadblocks should be performed before any advance study is made
    E. a roadblock operation can seldom be successfully undertaken by a single police agency

TEST 2

Questions 1-3.
DIRECTIONS: Answer Questions 1 to 3 *SOLELY* on the basis of the following statement:

All members of the police force must recognize that the people, through their representatives, hire and pay the police and that, as in any other employment, there must exist a proper employer-employee relationship. The police officer must understand that the essence of a correct police attitude is a willingness to serve, but at the same time he should distinguish between service and servility, and between courtesy and softness. He must be firm but also courteous, avoiding even an appearance of rudeness. He should develop a position that is friendly and unbiased, pleasant and sympathetic, in his relations with the general public, but firm and impersonal on occasions calling for regulation and control. A police officer should understand that his primary purpose is to prevent violations, not to arrest people. He should recognize the line of demarcation between a police function and passing judgment which is a court function. On the other side, a public that cooperates with the police, that supports them in their efforts and that observes laws and regulations may be said to have a desirable attitude.

1. In accordance with this paragraph, the *proper* attitude for a police officer to take is to
    A. be pleasant and sympathetic at all times
    B. be friendly, firm and impartial

C. be stern and severe in meting out justice to all
D. avoid being rude, except in those cases where the public is uncooperative

2. Assume that an officer is assigned by his superior officer to a busy traffic intersection and is warned to be on the lookout for motorists who skip the light or who are speeding.
According to this paragraph, it would be *proper* for the officer in this assignment to
   A. give a summons to every motorist whose car was crossing when the light changed
   B. hide behind a truck and wait for drivers who violate traffic laws
   C. select at random motorists who seem to be impatient and lecture them sternly on traffic safety
   D. stand on post in order to deter violations and give offenders a summons or a warning as required

3. According to this paragraph, a police officer must realize that the PRIMARY purpose of police work is to
   A. provide proper police service in a courteous manner
   B. decide whether those who violate the law should be punished
   C. arrest those who violate laws
   D. establish a proper employer-employee relationship

Questions 4-5.
DIRECTIONS: Answer Questions 4 and 5 SOLELY on the basis of the following statement:

If a motor vehicle fails to pass inspection, the owner will be given a rejection notice by the inspection station. Repairs must be made within ten days after this notice is issued. It is not necessary to have the required adjustment or repairs made at the station where the inspection occurred. The vehicle may be taken to any other garage. Re-inspection after repairs may be made at any official inspection station, not necessarily the same station which made the initial inspection. The registration of any motor vehicle for which an inspection sticker has not been obtained as required, or which is not repaired and inspected within ten days after inspection indicates defects, is subject to suspension. A vehicle cannot be used on public highways while its registration is under suspension.

4. According to the above paragraph, the owner of a car which does not pass inspection *must*
   A. have repairs made at the same station which rejected his car
   B. take the car to another station and have it re-inspected
   C. have repairs made anywhere and then have the car re-inspected
   D. not use the car on a public highway until the necessary repairs have been made

5. According to the above paragraph, the *one* of the following which may be cause for suspension of the registration of a vehicle is that
   A. an inspection sticker was issued before the rejection notice had been in force for ten days
   B. it was not re-inspected by the station that rejected it originally

C. it was not re-inspected either by the station that rejected it originally or by the garage which made the repairs
D. it has not had defective parts repaired within ten days after inspection

Questions 6-10.

DIRECTIONS: Answer Questions 6 to 10 *SOLELY* on the basis of the following statement:

If we are to study crime in its widest social setting, we will find a variety of conduct which, although criminal in the legal sense, is not offensive to the moral conscience of a considerable number of persons. Traffic violations, for example, do not brand the offender as guilty of moral offense. In fact, the recipient of a traffic ticket is usually simply the subject of some good natured joking by his friends. Although there may be indignation among certain groups of citizens against gambling and liquor law violations, these activities are often tolerated, if not openly supported, by the more numerous residents of the community. Indeed, certain social and service clubs regularly conduct gambling games and lotteries for the purpose of raising funds. Some communities regard violations involving the sale of liquor with little concern in order to profit from increased license fees and taxes paid by dealers. The thousand and one forms of political graft and corruption which infest our urban centers only occasionally arouse public condemnation and official action.

6. According to the above paragraph, *all* types of illegal conduct are
    A. condemned by all elements of the community
    B. considered a moral offense, although some are tolerated by a few citizens
    C. violations of the law, but some are acceptable to certain elements of the community
    D. found in a social setting which is not punishable by law

7. According to the above paragraph, traffic violations are *generally* considered by society as
    A. crimes requiring the maximum penalty set by the law
    B. more serious than violations of the liquor laws
    C. offenses against the morals of the community
    D. relatively minor offenses requiring minimum punishment

8. According to the above paragraph, a lottery conducted for the purpose of raising funds for a church
    A. is considered a serious violation of law
    B. may be tolerated by a community which has laws against gambling
    C. may be conducted under special laws demanded by the more numerous residents of a community
    D. arouses indignation in most communities

9. On the basis of the above paragraph, the *most likely* reaction in the community to a police raid on a gambling casino would be
    A. more an attitude of indifference than interest in the raid
    B. general approval of the raid
    C. condemnation of the raid by most people
    D. demand for further action, since this raid is not sufficient to end gambling activities

10. The one of the following which *BEST* describes the central thought of this paragraph and would be *MOST* suitable as a title for it is:
    A. Crime and the Police
    B. Public Condemnation of Graft and Corruption
    C. Gambling Is Not Always a Vicious Business
    D. Public Attitude toward Law Violations

Questions 11-13.

DIRECTIONS: Answer Questions 11-13 *SOLELY* on the basis of the following statement:

The law enforcement agency is one of the most important agencies in the field of juvenile delinquency prevention. This is so, not because of the social work connected with this problem, however, for this is not a police matter, but because the officers are usually the first to come in contact with the delinquent. The manner of arrest and detention makes a deep impression upon him and affects his life-long attitude toward society and the law. The juvenile court is perhaps the most important agency in this work. Contrary to the general opinion, however, it is not primarily concerned with putting children into correctional schools. The main purpose of the juvenile court is to save the child and to develop his emotional make-up, in order that he can grow up to be a decent and well-balanced citizen. The system of probation is the means whereby the court seeks to accomplish these goals.

11. According to this paragraph, police work is an *important* part of a program to prevent juvenile delinquency because
    A. social work is no longer considered important in juvenile delinquency prevention
    B. police officers are the first to have contact with the delinquent
    C. police officers jail the offender in order to be able to change his attitude toward society and the law
    D. it is the first step in placing the delinquent in jail

12. According to this paragraph, the *CHIEF* purpose of the juvenile court is to
    A. punish the child for his offense
    B. select a suitable correctional school for the delinquent
    C. use available means to help the delinquent become a better citizen
    D. provide psychiatric care for the delinquent

13. According to this paragraph, the juvenile court directs the development of delinquents under its care *CHIEFLY* by
    A. placing the child under probation
    B. sending the child to a correctional school
    C. keeping the delinquent in prison
    D. returning the child to his home

Questions 14-17.

DIRECTIONS: Answer Questions 14 to 17 *SOLELY* on the basis of the following statement:

When a vehicle has been disabled in the tunnel, the office on patrol in this zone should press the *emergency truck* light button. In the fast lane, red lights will go on throughout the tunnel; in the slow lane, amber lights will go on throughout the tunnel. The yellow zone light will go on at each signal control station throughout the tunnel and will flash the number of the zone in which the stoppage has occurred.

A red flashing pilot light will appear only at the signal control station at which the *emergency truck* button was pressed. The emergency garage will receive an audible and visual signal indicating the signal control station at which the *emergency truck* button was pressed. The garage officer shall acknowledge receipt of the signal by pressing the acknowledgment button. This will cause the pilot light at the operated signal control station in the tunnel to cease flashing and to remain steady. It is an answer to the officer at the operated signal control station that the emergency truck is responding to the call.

14. According to this paragraph, when the *emergency truck* light button is pressed
    A. amber lights will go on in every lane throughout the tunnel
    B. emergency signal lights will go on only in the lane in which the disabled vehicle happens to be
    C. red lights will go on in the fast lane throughout the tunnel
    D. pilot lights at all signal control stations will turn amber

15. According to this paragraph, the number of the zone in which the stoppage has occurred is flashed
    A. immediately after all the lights in the tunnel turn red
    B. by the yellow zone light at each signal control station
    C. by the emergency truck at the point of stoppage
    D. by the emergency garage

16. According to this paragraph, an officer near the disabled vehicle will know that the emergency tow truck is coming when
    A. the pilot light at the operated signal control station appears and flashes red
    B. an audible signal is heard in the tunnel
    C. the zone light at the operated signal control station turns red
    D. the pilot light at the operated signal control station becomes steady

17. Under the system described in the above paragraph, it would be *correct* to come to the conclusion that
    A. officers at all signal control stations are expected to acknowledge that they have received the stoppage signal
    B. officers at all signal control stations will know where the stoppage has occurred
    C. all traffic in both lanes of that side of the tunnel in which the stoppage has occurred must stop until the emergency truck has arrived
    D. there are two emergency garages, each able to respond to stoppages in traffic going in one particular direction

Questions 18-20.
DIRECTIONS: Answer Questions 18 to 20 *SOLELY* on the basis of the following statement:

In cases of accident it is most important for an officer to obtain the name, age, residence, occupation and a full description of the person injured, names and addresses of witnesses. He shall also obtain a statement of the attendant circumstances. He shall carefully note contributory conditions, if any, such as broken pavement, excavation, lights not burning, snow and ice on the roadway, etc. He shall

Test 2/3

enter all the facts in his memorandum book and on Form NY-17 or Form NY-18, and promptly transmit the original of the form to his superior officer and the duplicate to headquarters.

An officer shall render reasonable assistance to sick or injured persons. If the circumstances appear to require the services of a physician, he shall summon a physician by telephoning the superior officer on duty and notifying him of the apparent nature of the illness or accident and the location where the physician will be required. He may summon other officers to assist if circumstances warrant.

In case of an accident or where a person is sick on city property, an officer shall obtain the information necessary to fill out card Form NY-18 and record this in his memorandum book and promptly telephone the facts to his superior officer. He shall deliver the original card at the expiration of his tour to his superior officer and transmit the duplicate to headquarters.

18. According to this statement, the MOST important consideration in any report on a case of accident or injury is to
   A. obtain all the facts
   B. telephone his superior officer at once
   C. obtain a statement of the attendant circumstances
   D. determine ownership of the property on which the accident occurred

19. According to this statement, in the case of an accident on city property, the officer should *always*
   A. summon a physician before filling out any forms or making any entries in his memorandum book
   B. give his superior officer on duty a prompt report by telephone
   C. immediately bring the original of Form NY-18 to his superior officer on duty
   D. call at least one other officer to the scene to witness conditions

20. If the procedures stated were followed for all accidents in the city, an impartial survey of accidents occurring during any period of time in this city may be *most easily* made by
   A. asking a typical officer to show you his memorandum book
   B. having a superior officer investigate whether contributory conditions mentioned by witnesses actually exist
   C. checking all the records of all superior officers
   D. checking the duplicate card files at headquarters

TEST 3

Questions 1-3.
DIRECTIONS: Answer Questions 1 to 3 SOLELY on the basis of the following statement:

Modern police science may be said to have three phases. The first phase embraces the identification of living and dead persons. The second embraces the field work carried out by specially-trained detectives at the scene of the crime. The third embraces methods used in the police laboratory to examine and analyze clues and traces discovered in the course of the investigation. While modern police science has had a striking influence on detective work and will surely further enhance its effectiveness, the time-honored methods and practical detective work will always be important. The time-honored methods, that is, knowledge of methods used by criminals, patience, tact, industry, thoroughness, and imagination, will always be requisites for successful detective work.

1. According to the above statement, we may expect modern police science to
    A. help detective work more and more
    B. become more and more scientific
    C. depend less and less on the time-honored methods
    D. bring together the many different approaches to detective work
    E. play a less important role in detective work

2. According to the above statement, a knowledge of the procedures used by criminals is
    A. solely an element of the modern police science approach to detective work
    B. related to the identification of persons
    C. not related to detective field work
    D. related to methods used in the police laboratory
    E. an element of the traditional approach to detective work

3. Modern police science and practical detective work, according to the above statement,
    A. when used together, can only lead to confusion
    B. are based on distinctly different theories of detective work
    C. have had strikingly different influences on detective work
    D. should both be used for successful detective work
    E. lead usually to similar results

Questions 4-7.
DIRECTIONS: Answer Questions 4 to 7 *SOLELY* on the basis of the following statement:

A member of the force shall render reasonable aid to a sick or injured person. He shall summon an ambulance, if necessary, by telephoning the communications bureau of the county, who shall notify the precinct concerned. If possible, he shall wait in full view of the arriving ambulance and take necessary action to direct the responding doctor or attendant to the patient, without delay. If the ambulance does not arrive in twenty minutes, he shall send in a second call. However, if the sick person is in his or her own home, a member of the force, before summoning an ambulance, will ascertain whether such person is willing to be taken to a hospital for treatment.

4. According to the above statement, if a police officer wants to get an ambulance for a sick person, he should telephone
    A. the precinct concerned
    B. only if the sick person is in his home
    C. the nearest hospital
    D. only if the sick person is not in his home
    E. the county communications bureau

5. According to the above statement, if a police officer telephones for an ambulance and none arrives within twenty minutes, he should
   A. ask the injured person whether he is willing to be taken to a hospital
   B. call the county communications bureau
   C. call the precinct concerned
   D. attempt to give the injured person such assistance as he may need
   E. call the nearest hospital

6. A police officer is called to help a woman who has fallen in her own home and has apparently broken her leg. According to the above statement, he should
   A. ask her whether she wants to go to a hospital
   B. try to set her leg if it is necessary
   C. call for an ambulance at once
   D. attempt to get a doctor as quickly as possible
   E. not attempt to help the woman in any way before competent medical aid arrives

7. A man falls from a window into the backyard of an apartment house. Assume that you are a police officer and that you are called to assist this man.
   According to the above statement, after you have called for an ambulance and comforted the injured man as much as you can, you should
   A. wait in front of the house for the ambulance
   B. ask the injured man if he wishes to go to the hospital for treatment
   C. remain with the injured man until the ambulance arrives
   D. send a bystander to direct the nearest doctor to the patient
   E. not ask the man to explain how the accident happened

Questions 8-10.

DIRECTIONS: Answer Questions 8 to 10 *SOLELY* on the basis of the following statement.

What is required is a program that will protect our citizens and their property from criminal and antisocial acts, will effectively restrain and reform juvenile delinquents, and will prevent the further development of antisocial behavior. Discipline and punishment of offenders must necessarily play an important part in any such program. Serious offenders cannot be mollycoddled merely because they are under twenty-one. Restraint and punishment necessarily follow serious antisocial acts. But punishment, if it is to be effective, must be a planned part of a more comprehensive program of treating delinquency.

8. The *one* of the following goals *NOT* included among those listed above is to
   A. stop young people from defacing public property
   B. keep homes from being broken into
   C. develop an intra-city boys' baseball league
   D. change juvenile delinquents into useful citizens
   E. prevent young people from developing antisocial behavior patterns

9. According to the above statement, punishment is
    A. not satisfactory in any program dealing with juvenile delinquents
    B. the most effective means by which young vandals and hooligans can be reformed
    C. not used sufficiently when dealing with serious offenders who are under twenty-one
    D. of value in reducing juvenile delinquency only if it is part of a complete program
    E. most effective when it does not relate to specific antisocial acts

10. With respect to serious offenders who are under twenty-one, the above statement suggests that they
    A. be mollycoddled
    B. be dealt with as part of a comprehensive program to punish mature criminals
    C. should be punished
    D. be prevented, by brute force if necessary, from performing antisocial acts
    E. be treated as delinquent children who require more love than punishment

KEYS (CORRECT ANSWERS)

TEST 1	TEST 2	TEST 3
1. B	1. B	1. A
2. D	2. D	2. E
3. A	3. A	3. D
4. C	4. C	4. E
5. B	5. D	5. B
6. A	6. C	6. A
7. A	7. D	7. A
8. E	8. B	8. C
9. B	9. A	9. D
10. D	10. D	10. C
11. C	11. B	
12. C	12. C	
13. D	13. A	
14. B	14. C	
15. C	15. B	
16. E	16. D	
17. C	17. B	
18. E	18. A	
19. B	19. B	
20. C	20. D	

PREPARING WRITTEN MATERIAL

PARAGRAPH REARRANGEMENT
COMMENTARY

The sentences which follow are in scrambled order. You are to rearrange them in proper order and indicate the letter choice containing the correct answer at the space at the right.

Each group of sentences in this section is actually a paragraph presented in scrambled order. Each sentence in the group has a place in that paragraph; no sentence is to be left out. You are to read each group of sentences and decide upon the best order in which to put the sentences so as to form as well-organized paragraph.

The questions in this section measure the ability to solve a problem when all the facts relevant to its solution are not given.

More specifically, certain positions of responsibility and authority require the employee to discover connections between events sometimes, apparently, unrelated. In order to do this, the employee will find it necessary to correctly infer that unspecified events have probably occurred or are likely to occur. This ability becomes especially important when action must be taken on incomplete information.

Accordingly, these questions require competitors to choose among several suggested alternatives, each of which presents a different sequential arrangement of the events. Competitors must choose the MOST logical of the suggested sequences.

In order to do so, they may be required to draw on general knowledge to infer missing concepts or events that are essential to sequencing the given events. Competitors should be careful to infer only what is essential to the sequence. The plausibility of the wrong alternatives will always require the inclusion of unlikely events or of additional chains of events which are NOT essential to sequencing the given events.

It's very important to remember that you are looking for the best of the four possible choices, and that the best choice of all may not even be one of the answers you're given to choose from.

There is no one right way to these problems. Many people have found it helpful to first write out the order of the sentences, as they would have arranged them, on their scrap paper before looking at the possible answers. If their optimum answer is there, this can save them some time. If it isn't, this method can still give insight into solving the problem. Others find it most helpful to just go through each of the possible choices, contrasting each as they go along. You should use whatever method feels comfortable, and works, for you.

While most of these types of questions are not that difficult, we've added a higher percentage of the difficult type, just to give you more practice. Usually there are only one or two questions on this section that contain such subtle distinctions that you're unable to answer confidently, and you then may find yourself stuck deciding between two possible choices, neither of which you're sure about.

———

EXAMINATION SECTION
TEST 1

DIRECTIONS: Each question consists of several sentences which can be arranged in a logical sequence. For each question, select the choice which places the numbered sentences in the MOST logical sequence. *PRINT THE LETTER OF THE CORRECT ANSWER IN THE SPACE AT THE RIGHT.*

1.
   I. A body was found in the woods.
   II. A man proclaimed innocence.
   III. The owner of a gun was located.
   IV. A gun was traced.
   V. The owner of a gun was questioned.
   The CORRECT answer is:

   A. IV, III, V, II, I
   B. II, I, IV, III, V
   C. I, IV, III, V, II
   D. I, III, V, II, IV
   E. I, II, IV, III, V

   1.____

2.
   I. A man was in a hunting accident.
   I. A man fell down a flight of steps.
   II. A man lost his vision in one eye.
   III. A man broke his leg.
   IV. A man had to walk with a cane.
   The CORRECT answer is:

   A. II, IV, V, I, III
   B. IV, V, I, III, II
   C. III, I, IV, V, II
   D. I, III, V, II, IV
   E. I, III, II, IV, V

   2.____

3.
   I. A man is offered a new job.
   II. A woman is offered a new job.
   III. A man works as a waiter.
   IV. A woman works as a waitress.
   V. A woman gives notice.
   The CORRECT answer is:

   A. IV, II, V, III, I
   B. IV, II, V, I, III
   C. II, IV, V, III, I
   D. III, I, IV, II, V
   E. IV, III, II, V, I

   3.____

4.
   I. A train left the station late.
   II. A man was late for work.
   III. A man lost his job.
   IV. Many people complained because the train was late.
   V. There was a traffic jam.
   The CORRECT answer is:

   A. V, II, I, IV, III
   B. V, I, IV, II, III
   C. V, I, II, IV, III
   D. I, V, IV, II, III
   E. II, I, IV, V, III

   4.____

2 (#1)

5. I. The burden of proof as to each issue is determined before trial and remains upon the same party throughout the trial.
    II. The jury is at liberty to believe one witness' testimony as against a number of contradictory witnesses.
    III. In a civil case, the party bearing the burden of proof is required to prove his contention by a fair preponderance of the evidence.
    IV. However, it must be noted that a fair preponderance of evidence does not necessarily mean a greater number of witnesses.
    V. The burden of proof is the burden which rests upon one of the parties to an action to persuade the trier of the facts, generally the jury, that a proposition he asserts is true.
    VI. If the evidence is equally balanced, or if it leaves the jury in such doubt as to be unable to decide the controversy either way, judgment must be given against the party upon whom the burden of proof rests.
    The CORRECT answer is:

    A. III, II, V, IV, I, VI
    B. I, II, VI, V, III, IV
    C. III, IV, V, I, II, VI
    D. V, I, III, VI, IV, II
    E. I, V, III, VI, IV, II

5.____

6. I. If a parent is without assets and is unemployed, he cannot be convicted of the crime of non-support of a child.
    II. The term *sufficient ability* has been held to mean sufficient financial ability.
    III. It does not matter if his unemployment is by choice or unavoidable circumstances.
    IV. If he fails to take any steps at all, he may be liable to prosecution for endangering the welfare of a child.
    V. Under the penal law, a parent is responsible for the support of his minor child only if the parent is *of* sufficient ability.
    VI. An indigent parent may meet his obligation by borrowing money or by seeking aid under the provisions of the Social Welfare Law.
    The CORRECT answer is:

    A. VI, I, V, III, II, IV
    B. I, III, V, II, IV, VI
    C. V, II, I, III, VI, IV
    D. I, VI, IV, V, II, III
    E. II, V, I, III, VI, IV

6.____

7. I. Consider, for example, the case of a rabble rouser who urges a group of twenty people to go out and break the windows of a nearby factory.
    II. Therefore, the law fills the indicated gap with the crime of *inciting to riot*.
    III. A person is considered guilty of inciting to riot when he urges ten or more persons to engage in tumultuous and violent conduct of a kind likely to create public alarm.
    IV. However, if he has not obtained the cooperation of at least four people, he cannot be charged with unlawful assembly.
    V. The charge of inciting to riot was added to the law to cover types of conduct which cannot be classified as either the crime of *riot* or the crime of *unlawful assembly*.
    VI. If he acquires the acquiescence of at least four of them, he is guilty of unlawful assembly even if the project does not materialize.
    The CORRECT answer is:

7.____

A. III, V, I, VI, IV, II		B. V, I, IV, VI, II, III	
C. III, IV, I, V, II, VI		D. V, I, IV, VI, III, II	
E. V, III, I, VI, IV, II			

8. I. If, however, the rebuttal evidence presents an issue of credibility, it is for the jury to determine whether the presumption has, in fact, been destroyed.   8.____
    II. Once sufficient evidence to the contrary is introduced, the presumption disappears from the trial.
    III. The effect of a presumption is to place the burden upon the adversary to come forward with evidence to rebut the presumption.
    IV. When a presumption is overcome and ceases to exist in the case, the fact or facts which gave rise to the presumption still remain.
    V. Whether a presumption has been overcome is ordinarily a question for the court.
    VI. Such information may furnish a basis for a logical inference.
    The CORRECT answer is:

    A. IV, VI, II, V, I, III   B. III, II, V, I, IV, VI
    C. V, III, VI, IV, II, I   D. V, IV, I, II, VI, III
    E. II, III, V, I, IV, VI

9. I. An executive may answer a letter by writing his reply on the face of the letter itself instead of having a return letter typed.   9.____
    II. This procedure is efficient because it saves the executive's time, the typist's time, and saves office file space.
    III. Copying machines are used in small offices as well as large offices to save time and money in making brief replies to business letters.
    IV. A copy is made on a copying machine to go into the company files, while the original is mailed back to the sender.
    The CORRECT answer is:

    A. I, II, IV, III   B. I, IV, II, III
    C. III, I, IV, II   D. III, IV, II, I

10. I. Most organizations favor one of the types but always include the others to a lesser degree.   10.____
    II. However, we can detect a definite trend toward greater use of symbolic control.
    III. We suggest that our local police agencies are today primarily utilizing material control.
    IV. Control can be classified into three types: physical, material, and symbolic.
    The CORRECT answer is:

    A. IV, II, III, I   B. II, I, IV, III
    C. III, IV, II, I   D. IV, I, III, II

11. I. Project residents had first claim to this use, followed by surrounding neighborhood children.   11.____
    II. By contrast, recreation space within the project's interior was found to be used more often by both groups.
    III. Studies of the use of project grounds in many cities showed grounds left open for public use were neglected and unused, both by residents and by members of the surrounding community.

IV. Project residents had clearly laid claim to the play spaces, setting up and enforcing unwritten rules for use.
V. Each group, by experience, found their activities easily disrupted by other groups, and their claim to the use of space for recreation difficult to enforce.

The CORRECT answer is:

A. IV, V, I, II, III
B. V, II, IV, III, I
C. I, IV, III, II, V
D. III, V, II, IV, I

12.
I. They do not consider the problems correctable within the existing subsidy formula and social policy of accepting all eligible applicants regardless of social behavior and lifestyle.
II. A recent survey, however, indicated that tenants believe these problems correctable by local housing authorities and management within the existing financial formula.
III. Many of the problems and complaints concerning public housing management and design have created resentment between the tenant and the landlord.
IV. This same survey indicated that administrators and managers do not agree with the tenants.

The CORRECT answer is:

A. II, I, III, IV
B. I, III, IV, II
C. III, II, IV, I
D. IV, II, I, III

13.
I. In single-family residences, there is usually enough distance between tenants to prevent occupants from annoying one another.
II. For example, a certain small percentage of tenant families has one or more members addicted to alcohol.
III. While managers believe in the right of individuals to live as they choose, the manager becomes concerned when the pattern of living jeopardizes others' rights.
IV. Still others turn night into day, staging lusty entertainments which carry on into the hours when most tenants are trying to sleep.
V. In apartment buildings, however, tenants live so closely together that any misbehavior can result in unpleasant living conditions.
VI. Other families engage in violent argument.

The CORRECT answer is:

A. III, II, V, IV, VI, I
B. I, V, II, VI, IV, III
C. II, V, IV, I, III, VI
D. IV, II, V, VI, III, I

14.
I. Congress made the commitment explicit in the Housing Act of 1949, establishing as a national goal the realization of *a decent home and suitable environment for every American family.*
II. The result has been that the goal of decent home and suitable environment is still as far distant as ever for the disadvantaged urban family.
III. In spite of this action by Congress, federal housing programs have continued to be fragmented and grossly underfunded.
IV. The passage of the National Housing Act signalled a new federal commitment to provide housing for the nation's citizens.

The CORRECT answer is:

A. I, IV, III, II
B. IV, I, III, II
C. IV, I, II, III
D. II, IV, I, III

15. I. The greater expense does not necessarily involve *exploitation,* but it is often perceived as exploitative and unfair by those who are aware of the price differences involved, but unaware of operating costs.
II. Ghetto residents believe they are *exploited* by local merchants, and evidence substantiates some of these beliefs.
III. However, stores in low-income areas were more likely to be small independents, which could not achieve the economies available to supermarket chains and were, therefore, more likely to charge higher prices, and the customers were more likely to buy smaller-sized packages which are more expensive per unit of measure.
IV. A study conducted in one city showed that distinctly higher prices were charged for goods sold in ghetto stores than in other areas.

The CORRECT answer is:

A. IV, II, I, III
B. IV, I, III, II
C. II, IV, III, I
D. II, III, IV, I

KEY (CORRECT ANSWERS)

1. C
2. E
3. B
4. D
5. D

6. C
7. A
8. B
9. C
10. D

11. D
12. C
13. B
14. B
15. C

PREPARING WRITTEN MATERIAL
EXAMINATION SECTION

Test 1/2

TEST 1

DIRECTIONS: The sentences numbered 1 to 10 deal with some phase of police activity. They may be classified most appropriately under one of the following four categories:
  A. *Faulty* because of incorrect grammar
  B. *Faulty* because of incorrect punctuation
  C. *Faulty* because of incorrect use of a word
  D. *Correct*

Examine each sentence carefully. Then, in the correspondingly numbered space on the right, print the capital letter preceding the option which is the best of the four suggested above.

(All incorrect sentences contain only one type of error. Consider a sentence correct if it contains none of the types of errors mentioned, even though there may be other correct ways of expressing the same thought.)

1. The Department Medal of Honor is awarded to a member of the Police Force who distinguishes himself inconspicuously in the line of police duty by the performance of an act of gallantry.   1. ...

2. Members of the Detective Division are charged with: the prevention of crime, the detection and arrest of criminals, and the recovery of lost or stolen property.   2. ...

3. Detectives are selected from the uniformed patrol forces after they have indicated by conduct, aptitude, and performance that they are qualified for the more intricate duties of a detective.   3. ...

4. The patrolman, pursuing his assailant, exchanged shots with the gunman and immortally wounded him as he fled into a nearby building.   4. ...

5. The members of the Traffic Division has to enforce the Vehicle and Traffic Law, the Traffic Regulations, and ordinances relating to vehicular and pedestrian traffic.   5. ...

6. After firing a shot at the gunman, the crowd dispersed from the patrolman's line of fire.   6. ...

7. The efficiency of the Missing Persons Bureau is maintained with a maximum of public personnel due to the specialized training given to its members.   7. ...

8. Records of persons arrested for violations of Vehicle and Traffic Regulations are transmitted upon request to precincts, courts and other authorized agencies.   8. ...

9. The arresting officer done all he could to subdue the perpetrator without physically injuring him.   9. ...

10. The Deputy Commissioner is authorized to exercise all of the powers and duties of the Police Commissioner in the latter's absence.   10. ...

TEST 2

DIRECTIONS: Questions 1 through 4 consist of sentences concerning criminal law. Some of the sentences contain errors in English grammar or usage, punctuation, spelling or capitalization. (A sentence does not contain an error simply because it could be written in a different manner.)

Choose answer
- A. if the sentence contains an error in English grammar or usage
- B. if the sentence contains an error in punctuation
- C. if the sentence contains an error in spelling or capitalization
- D. if the sentence does not contain any errors

1. The severity of the sentence prescribed by contemporary statutes - including both the former and the revised New York Penal Laws - do not depend on what crime was intended by the offender.   1. ...

2. It is generally recognized that two defects in the early law of attempt played a part in the birth of burglary: (1) immunity from prosecution for conduct short of the last act before completion of the crime, and (2) the relatively minor penalty imposed for an attempt (it being a common law misdemeanor) vis-a-vis the completed offense.   2. ...

3. The first sentence of the statute is applicable to employees who enter their place of employment, invited guests, and all other persons who have an express or implied license or privilege to enter the premises.   3. ...

4. Contemporary criminal codes in the United States generally divide burglary into various degrees, differentiating the categories according to place, time and other attendent circumstances.   4. ...

TEST 3

DIRECTIONS: For each of the sentences numbered 1 through 10, select from the options given below the *MOST* applicable choice, and print the letter of the correct answer in the space at the right.
- A. The sentence is correct
- B. The sentence contains a spelling error only
- C. The sentence contains an English grammar error only
- D. The sentence contains *both* a spelling error and an English grammar error

1. Every person in the group is going to do his share.   1. ...
2. The man who we selected is new to this University.   2. ...
3. She is the older of the four secretaries on the two staffs that are to be combined.   3. ...
4. The decision has to be made between him and I.   4. ...
5. One of the volunteers are too young for this complecated task, don't you think?   5. ...
6. I think your idea is splindid and it will improve this report considerably.   6. ...
7. Do you think this is an exagerated account of the behavior you and me observed this morning?   7. ...
8. Our supervisor has a clear idea of excelence.   8. ...
9. How many occurences were verified by the observers?   9. ...
10. We must complete the typing of the draft of the questionaire by noon tomorrow.   10. ...

TEST 4

DIRECTIONS: Questions 1 through 3 are based on the following paragraph, which consists of three numbered sentences.
Edit each sentence to insure clarity of meaning and correctness of grammar without substantially changing the meaning of the sentence.

Examine each sentence and then select the option which changes the sentence to express *BEST* the thought of the sentence.

(1) Unquestionably, a knowledge of business and finance is a good advantage to audit committee members but not essential to all members. (2) Other factors also carry weight; for example, at least one member must have the ability to preside over meetings and to discuss things along constructive lines. (3) In the same way, such factors as the amount of time a member can be able to devote to duties or his rating on the score of motivation, inquisitiveness, persistence, and disposition towards critical analysis are important.

1. In the first sentence, the word 1. ...
   A. "good" should be changed to "distinct"
   B. "good" should be omitted
   C. "and" should be changed to "or"
   D. "are" should be inserted between the words "but" and "not"
2. In the second sentence, the 2. ...
   A. word "factors" should be changed to "things"
   B. words "preside over" should be changed to "lead at"
   C. phrase "discuss things" should be changed to "direct the discussion"
   D. word "constructive" should be changed to "noteworthy"
3. In the third sentence, the 3. ...
   A. word "amount" should be changed to "period"
   B. words "amount of" should be changed to "length of"
   C. word "can" should be changed to "will"
   D. word "same" should be changed to "similar"

DIRECTIONS FOR TESTS 5-6: Each question or incomplete statement is followed by several suggested answers or completions. Select the one that *BEST* answers the question or completes the statement. Print the letter of the correct answer in the space at the right.

TEST 5

1. Of the following, the *MOST* acceptable close of a business letter would usually be: 1. ...
   A. Cordially yours,   B. Respectfully Yours,
   C. Sincerely Yours,   D. Yours very truly,
2. When writing official correspondence to members of the armed forces, their titles should be used 2. ...
   A. both on the envelope and in the inside address
   B. in the inside address, but not on the envelope
   C. neither on the envelope nor in the inside address
   D. on the envelope but not in the inside address
3. *Which one* of the following is the *LEAST* important advantage of putting the subject of a letter in the heading to the right of the address? It 3. ...
   A. makes filing of the copy easier
   B. makes more space available in the body of the letter
   C. simplifies distribution of letters
   D. simplifies determination of the subject of the letter
4. Generally, when writing a letter, the use of precise words and concise sentences is 4. ...
   A. *good*, because less time will be required to write the letter
   B. *bad*, because it is most likely that the reader will think the letter is unimportant and will not respond favorably

C. *good,* because it is likely that your desired meaning will be conveyed to the reader
D. *bad,* because your letter will be too brief to provide adequate information

5. Of the following, it is MOST appropriate to use a form letter when it is necessary to answer *many*
   A. requests or inquiries from a single individual
   B. follow-up letters from individuals requesting additional information
   C. requests or inquiries about a single subject
   D. complaints from individuals that they have been unable to obtain various types of information

TEST 6

1. The *one* of the following sentences which is LEAST acceptable from the viewpoint of correct usage is:
   A. The police thought the fugitive to be him.
   B. The criminals set a trap for whoever would fall into it.
   C. It is ten years ago since the fugitive fled from the city.
   D. The lecturer argued that criminals are usually cowards.
   E. The police removed four bucketfuls of earth from the scene of the crime.

2. The *one* of the following sentences which is LEAST acceptable from the viewpoint of correct usage is:
   A. The patrolman scrutinized the report with great care.
   B. Approaching the victim of the assault, two bruises were noticed by the patrolman.
   C. As soon as I had broken down the door, I stepped into the room.
   D. I observed the accused loitering near the building, which was closed at the time.
   E. The storekeeper complained that his neighbor was guilty of violating a local ordinance.

3. The *one* of the following sentences which is LEAST acceptable from the viewpoint of correct usage is:
   A. I realized immediately that he intended to assault the woman, so I disarmed him.
   B. It was apparent that Mr. Smith's explanation contained many inconsistencies.
   C. Despite the slippery condition of the street, he managed to stop the vehicle before injuring the child.
   D. Not a single one of them wish, despite the damage to property, to make a formal complaint.
   E. The body was found lying on the floor.

KEY (CORRECT ANSWERS)

TEST 1		TEST 2	TEST 3		TEST 4	TEST 5	TEST 6
1. C	6. A	1. A	1. A	6. B	1. A	1. D	1. C
2. B	7. C	2. D	2. C	7. D	2. C	2. A	2. B
3. D	8. D	3. D	3. C	8. B	3. C	3. B	3. D
4. C	9. A	4. C	4. C	9. B		4. C	
5. A	10. D		5. D	10. B		5. C	

PREPARING WRITTEN MATERIAL
Test 1/2
EXAMINATION SECTION
TEST 1

DIRECTIONS: The sentences numbered 1 to 10 deal with some phase of police activity. They may be classified most appropriately under one of the following four categories:
  A. *Faulty* because of incorrect grammar
  B. *Faulty* because of incorrect punctuation
  C. *Faulty* because of incorrect use of a word
  D. *Correct*

Examine each sentence carefully. Then, in the correspondingly numbered space on the right, print the capital letter preceding the option which is the best of the four suggested above.

(All incorrect sentences contain only one type of error. Consider a sentence correct if it contains none of the types of errors mentioned, even though there may be other correct ways of expressing the same thought.)

1. The Department Medal of Honor is awarded to a member of the Police Force who distinguishes himself inconspicuously in the line of police duty by the performance of an act of gallantry.   1. ...

2. Members of the Detective Division are charged with: the prevention of crime, the detection and arrest of criminals, and the recovery of lost or stolen property.   2. ...

3. Detectives are selected from the uniformed patrol forces after they have indicated by conduct, aptitude, and performance that they are qualified for the more intricate duties of a detective.   3. ...

4. The patrolman, pursuing his assailant, exchanged shots with the gunman and immortally wounded him as he fled into a nearby building.   4. ...

5. The members of the Traffic Division has to enforce the Vehicle and Traffic Law, the Traffic Regulations, and ordinances relating to vehicular and pedestrian traffic.   5. ...

6. After firing a shot at the gunman, the crowd dispersed from the patrolman's line of fire.   6. ...

7. The efficiency of the Missing Persons Bureau is maintained with a maximum of public personnel due to the specialized training given to its members.   7. ...

8. Records of persons arrested for violations of Vehicle and Traffic Regulations are transmitted upon request to precincts, courts and other authorized agencies.   8. ...

9. The arresting officer done all he could to subdue the perpetrator without physically injuring him.   9. ...

10. The Deputy Commissioner is authorized to exercise all of the powers and duties of the Police Commissioner in the latter's absence.   10. ...

TEST 2

DIRECTIONS: Questions 1 through 4 consist of sentences concerning criminal law. Some of the sentences contain errors in English grammar or usage, punctuation, spelling or capitalization. (A sentence does not contain an error simply because it could be written in a different manner.)

Choose answer
- A. if the sentence contains an error in English grammar or usage
- B. if the sentence contains an error in punctuation
- C. if the sentence contains an error in spelling or capitalization
- D. if the sentence does not contain any errors

1. The severity of the sentence prescribed by contemporary statutes - including both the former and the revised New York Penal Laws - do not depend on what crime was intended by the offender.   1. ...
2. It is generally recognized that two defects in the early law of attempt played a part in the birth of burglary: (1) immunity from prosecution for conduct short of the last act before completion of the crime, and (2) the relatively minor penalty imposed for an attempt (it being a common law misdemeanor) vis-a-vis the completed offense.   2. ...
3. The first sentence of the statute is applicable to employees who enter their place of employment, invited guests, and all other persons who have an express or implied license or privilege to enter the premises.   3. ...
4. Contemporary criminal codes in the United States generally divide burglary into various degrees, differentiating the categories according to place, time and other attendent circumstances.   4. ...

TEST 3

DIRECTIONS: For each of the sentences numbered 1 through 10, select from the options given below the *MOST* applicable choice, and print the letter of the correct answer in the space at the right.
- A. The sentence is correct
- B. The sentence contains a spelling error only
- C. The sentence contains an English grammar error only
- D. The sentence contains *both* a spelling error and an English grammar error

1. Every person in the group is going to do his share.   1. ...
2. The man who we selected is new to this University.   2. ...
3. She is the older of the four secretaries on the two staffs that are to be combined.   3. ...
4. The decision has to be made between him and I.   4. ...
5. One of the volunteers are too young for this complecated task, don't you think?   5. ...
6. I think your idea is splindid and it will improve this report considerably.   6. ...
7. Do you think this is an exagerated account of the behavior you and me observed this morning?   7. ...
8. Our supervisor has a clear idea of excelence.   8. ...
9. How many occurences were verified by the observers?   9. ...
10. We must complete the typing of the draft of the questionaire by noon tomorrow.   10. ...

TEST 4

DIRECTIONS: Questions 1 through 3 are based on the following paragraph, which consists of three numbered sentences.
Edit each sentence to insure clarity of meaning and correctness of grammar without substantially changing the meaning of the sentence.

Examine each sentence and then select the option which changes the sentence to express BEST the thought of the sentence.

(1) Unquestionably, a knowledge of business and finance is a good advantage to audit committee members but not essential to all members. (2) Other factors also carry weight; for example, at least one member must have the ability to preside over meetings and to discuss things along constructive lines. (3) In the same way, such factors as the amount of time a member can be able to devote to duties or his rating on the score of motivation, inquisitiveness, persistence, and disposition towards critical analysis are important.

1. In the first sentence, the word
   A. "good" should be changed to "distinct"
   B. "good" should be omitted
   C. "and" should be changed to "or"
   D. "are" should be inserted between the words "but" and "not"
2. In the second sentence, the
   A. word "factors" should be changed to "things"
   B. words "preside over" should be changed to "lead at"
   C. phrase "discuss things" should be changed to "direct the discussion"
   D. word "constructive" should be changed to "noteworthy"
3. In the third sentence, the
   A. word "amount" should be changed to "period"
   B. words "amount of" should be changed to "length of"
   C. word "can" should be changed to "will"
   D. word "same" should be changed to "similar"

DIRECTIONS FOR TESTS 5-6: Each question or incomplete statement is followed by several suggested answers or completions. Select the one that BEST answers the question or completes the statement. Print the letter of the correct answer in the space at the right.

TEST 5

1. Of the following, the MOST acceptable close of a business letter would usually be:
   A. Cordially yours,   B. Respectfully Yours,
   C. Sincerely Yours,   D. Yours very truly,
2. When writing official correspondence to members of the armed forces, their titles should be used
   A. both on the envelope and in the inside address
   B. in the inside address, but not on the envelope
   C. neither on the envelope nor in the inside address
   D. on the envelope but not in the inside address
3. Which one of the following is the LEAST important advantage of putting the subject of a letter in the heading to the right of the address? It
   A. makes filing of the copy easier
   B. makes more space available in the body of the letter
   C. simplifies distribution of letters
   D. simplifies determination of the subject of the letter
4. Generally, when writing a letter, the use of precise words and concise sentences is
   A. *good*, because less time will be required to write the letter
   B. *bad*, because it is most likely that the reader will think the letter is unimportant and will not respond favorably

C. *good,* because it is likely that your desired meaning will be conveyed to the reader
D. *bad,* because your letter will be too brief to provide adequate information

5. Of the following, it is MOST appropriate to use a form letter when it is necessary to answer *many*
   A. requests or inquiries from a single individual
   B. follow-up letters from individuals requesting additional information
   C. requests or inquiries about a single subject
   D. complaints from individuals that they have been unable to obtain various types of information

TEST 6

1. The *one* of the following sentences which is LEAST acceptable from the viewpoint of correct usage is:
   A. The police thought the fugitive to be him.
   B. The criminals set a trap for whoever would fall into it.
   C. It is ten years ago since the fugitive fled from the city.
   D. The lecturer argued that criminals are usually cowards.
   E. The police removed four bucketfuls of earth from the scene of the crime.

2. The *one* of the following sentences which is LEAST acceptable from the viewpoint of correct usage is:
   A. The patrolman scrutinized the report with great care.
   B. Approaching the victim of the assault, two bruises were noticed by the patrolman.
   C. As soon as I had broken down the door, I stepped into the room.
   D. I observed the accused loitering near the building, which was closed at the time.
   E. The storekeeper complained that his neighbor was guilty of violating a local ordinance.

3. The *one* of the following sentences which is LEAST acceptable from the viewpoint of correct usage is:
   A. I realized immediately that he intended to assault the woman, so I disarmed him.
   B. It was apparent that Mr. Smith's explanation contained many inconsistencies.
   C. Despite the slippery condition of the street, he managed to stop the vehicle before injuring the child.
   D. Not a single one of them wish, despite the damage to property, to make a formal complaint.
   E. The body was found lying on the floor.

KEY (CORRECT ANSWERS)

TEST 1		TEST 2	TEST 3		TEST 4	TEST 5	TEST 6
1. C	6. A	1. A	1. A	6. B	1. A	1. D	1. C
2. B	7. C	2. D	2. C	7. D	2. C	2. A	2. B
3. D	8. D	3. D	3. C	8. B	3. C	3. B	3. D
4. C	9. A	4. C	4. C	9. B		4. C	
5. A	10. D		5. D	10. B		5. C	

CAMPUS SECURITY

COMMENTARY

This section describes the structure of the campus security office and appraises its function through an examination of its legal apparatus and by the relationships it has maintained with other components of institutional life.

The findings are based upon research in the legal status of the security office and the authority of the security officer; questions as to the structure, the functioning, and the relationships of the security office; and the assessment of the campus security function and its ability to be supportive to students.

In particular, this summary takes cognizance of the inconsequential role heretofore delegated to the security officer and the significant part he may yet play as the threat to the security of the campus accelerates.

---

1. The history of the campus security office reflects a variety of service tasks distributed among several functionaries which ultimately came to be housed together. From the early fire-watching days to traffic control and student disorder, it has been a body generally utilized "for" but rarely considered "of" the university. Campus security officers and their predecessors have been long cast in roles of menial activities with minimal responsibilities. Never having attained recognition and legitimacy as a part of the total university community, they continue to exercise an uncertain authority amidst a questioning constituency.

2. The uncertainty that has always surrounded the role of the campus security officer is best evidenced in the limitations placed upon his authority. Until recent years few of the state legislatures bestowed direct arrest authority upon a campus security officer. The authority was obtained derivatively as a result of deputization by the local municipal police department or by the sheriff. Although many state legislatures now permit the governing bodies of higher education, such as the boards of regents, to designate campus security officers with peace officers' authority, deputization continues.

3. This situation exists inasmuch as the authority obtained through the governing bodies is usually of a narrow range and it has not yet had the benefit of adequate court testing and judicial approval. Some few states permit private colleges to obtain similar appointments, generally through application to the governor, but the rule among private colleges has been to rely on deputization for their campus security authority.

4. Among the states requiring mandatory training for entering police officers, several do not yet consider a campus security officer subject to the standards imposed upon peace officers. Moreover, the federal government specifically excludes many campus security officers from the benefits of available training scholarships. Virtually no organized, state-wide specialized training programs for campus security officers are either required under the law or are afforded under state auspices.

5. The law is well established in regard the right of institutions of higher educations to control traffic and parking within their own disciplinary machinery. The courts have upheld the colleges' imposition of reasonable penalties for such violations and have provided the civil court system as an appeal tribunal.

6. Adequate legal precedent exists upon which a campus security officer may enter a residence hall in search of contraband without benefit of a search warrant. The case law condoning such entry is predicated upon several theories. The major legal premise is that the institution must be afforded the flexibility of access to all buildings in order to properly govern itself. The student is also considered only a temporary occupant of the premises and by his enrollment "waives" certain rights. The privilege of entry is available to administrators and may be delegated to law enforcement officers in the pursuit of a reasonable investigation. The erosion of the "in loco parentis" doctrine and recent judicial pronouncements suggest that the privilege of entry without a warrant may not be arbitrarily invoked.

7. The formalized role of the campus security office in major stress situations such as organized or spontaneous campus disorder is to provide intelligence upon which administrators may make decisions, to serve as liaison with outside police agencies, and to gather evidence for later use against students violating the law. Although the press of events may force campus security officers into confrontation situations, the plans for responding to campus disorders do not generally contemplate such a role. The campus security office's early involvement is aimed primarily at delay so that student personnel officers and the executive officer may have the opportunity to use whatever personal, persuasive influence they can marshal. In the event the institutional executive determines that outside force is necessary, the campus security serves as a communications liaison to interpret the tactical decisions demanded by the outside police agencies in terms of the goals aspired to by the executive.

8. While the complexities of a campus-wide disorder may impose limitations upon the involvement of the security officer, his ability to respond to the normal, foreseeable, routine, enforcement contingencies also remains open to question. The profile of the campus security function discloses many characteristics that suggest only a minimal ability to satisfy ordinary campus needs.

9. Particularly among small institutions and especially private colleges, the training is limited, the equipment is meager, and the advantages over the local police non-existent. The security force generally lacks specialists within the department, has a minimum of sophisticated equipment, and what little intelligence is available is obtained from outside police sources. Students and female officers are scarcely used and only in short demand.

10. All components of the university recognize that the campus security force most effectively performs the tasks requiring the least specialty training. Building and ground patrol, parking, and traffic control are at the top rank, in that order, while the duties involving criminal investigation and student disorders are the areas least effectively performed.

11. It is apparent to security officers that the presence of larger student bodies, more vehicles on campus, more buildings to patrol, a rise in the individual crime rate, and the potential for disorder arising from student demonstrations call for an increased professional staff.

12. Administrative changes are sought by security officers with almost 60.0 percent favoring a centralized, state-wide coordinating body and almost 70.0 percent requesting a chain of command which

would lead directly to the president. None of the other respondent groups (faculty, students, administrators) evinces strong support for these propositions.

13. There is no consensus among the campus groups as to the personnel changes which would most improve performance. The security officers and the administrators ranked salary increase as the top priority personnel change, whereas the students and the faculty selected specialized training in human behavior as their first choice. Inasmuch as the campus security office services a select clientele in a unique setting, the projected changes need not be weighed against the prototype sought for the law enforcement officer employed to exercise order among the general population.

14. The campus security office has virtually no involvement in policy-making beyond traffic regulations and has little contact in a formal setting with students and faculty. A good working relationship seems to exist with the office of student affairs and other administrators as well as with the outside police agencies.

15. The strong support indicated by all four groups (campus security, faculty, students, and administrators) for the proposition that too few channels of communication exist between the campus security office and the students is evidenced by the lack of security officer participation in student educational programs, by the failure of the campus security office to meet regularly with student committees, and by the security office's absence in the process of establishing student codes of conduct and student discipline procedures. Students involved in off-campus arrests cannot look for security office assistance except to a small extent at schools in the under-10,000 population brackets.

16. Although administrative support for the campus security office as a policy-making body is absent, there is evidence showing regular committee meetings with the office of student affairs and other administration groups. A continuing exchange of information exists with the office of student affairs concerning problem students, and a concurring belief is held by all four groups that the administrators and the office of student affairs would support the action of the campus security office in a disorder situation.

17. The working relationship with administrators also extends to outside police agencies. The local police are available for many manpower and investigative services, and, in some instances, campus violations of the municipal and state law may be handled by security officers within the framework of the school's discipline structure rather than requiring students to face criminal prosecution. Despite the amicable ties between the campus security force and the local police, the security officer joined with the other three groups in unequivocally asserting that the over-reaction by outside police agencies was the occurrence most likely to change an orderly student demonstration into a campus disorder.

18. The aspirations of the campus security officer to contribute to the educational goals of the institution and to participate in its traditional customs finds little of a responsive chord among other components on campus. Although 40.0 percent of the security officers considered the aiding of students in the educational process as an appropriate goal, only 18.0 percent of the students and 6.0 percent of the faculty voiced agreement. The campus security officer viewed himself as the interpreter of the function of police agencies in our

society, but the concept had only scattered support with the students and the faculty.

19. There was mixed sentiment toward the campus security officer's enforcement role. Some of the characteristics deemed the antithesis of higher education tradition were attributed to him. For instance, all of the groups identified him with an authoritarian enforcement approach. In addition, 50.0 percent of the student were critical of his use of informers and about 25.0 percent of all groups suggested that uniforms be replaced with civilian-like attire. Despite the 70.0 percent of the security officers seeking increased authority, there was a reluctance to increase campus security authority or to allow participation in student discipline policy-making. The suggestion that the campus security office is a policing agency and as such is unacceptable to the academic community averaged but a 30.0 percent acceptance among all four groups. While the campus security office was not totally repudiated because of its law enforcement posture, nonetheless it has not been afforded peer status by the other components of the campus society.

20. The anticipation that a supportive relationship can be maintained with students while performing enforcement duties is an unfulfilled expectation. This was apparent to all four groups in their over-70.0 percent recognition that duties such as searching residence halls for contraband are inimical to maintaining a compatible association, and, as well, in their almost 50.0 percent recognition of the stress created in using necessary force against student disorders. Duties involving building and grounds patrol, traffic control, and criminal investigation are performed in less strained settings, permitting a more harmonious relationship.

21. The image of the campus security officer that is transmitted to the student represents order and authority. The uniform, the weapons, and the equipment are synonymous with discipline and control. From the student point of view, the product is not conducive to a mutuality of interest. The absence of joint educational programs and regularly scheduled committee meetings also negates the development of any meaningful interchange. The failure of campus security to offer assistance to students in need of aid as a result of an off-campus arrest may further estrange the two groups. The differential in educational background and age also widens the chasm.

22. Students do not go so far as to state that the campus security officer is too low in the status hierarchy to maintain their respect but they strongly favor supervisory controls such as student ombudsmen and a joint faculty-student committee to review the performance of the campus security officer.

23. The campus security officer as presently constituted is not trained to provide supportive services for students, is not given a status role by the administration which would engender a high regard, and does not participate in policy making or become involved in aspects of the educational process.

24. Little recognition is attainable to the security officer other than that arising from his enforcement activities. There are few if any common grounds existing between him and the student from which a symbiotic relationship may develop.

25. In some few critical areas, the results reflected similar percentage support among the four groups. However, the internal consistency check to determine agreement among the four groups within

each institution showed that in only 2 of the 16 selected items were there affirmative responses suggesting consistent agreement within each of the schools. The item of greatest support had 82 of the 89 schools with all four groups agreeing to the truism that the campus security goal is to provide protection for property and person. Fifty schools had all components in agreement that the over-reaction by outside police agencies may change orderly demonstrations into a campus disorder. **The other items** showed considerably lower internal consistency scores. The diversity of attitude among the component groups that comprise the educational institutions of higher learning and the lack of unanimity within each institution suggest a searching reexamination of the campus security model.

ANSWER SHEET

TEST NO. ____________ PART ______ TITLE OF POSITION ______________________________
(AS GIVEN IN EXAMINATION ANNOUNCEMENT - INCLUDE OPTION, IF ANY)

PLACE OF EXAMINATION ______________________________ ______________ DATE ____________
(CITY OR TOWN) (STATE)

RATING

USE THE SPECIAL PENCIL. MAKE GLOSSY BLACK MARKS.

1 A B C D E	26 A B C D E	51 A B C D E	76 A B C D E	101 A B C D E
2 A B C D E	27 A B C D E	52 A B C D E	77 A B C D E	102 A B C D E
3 A B C D E	28 A B C D E	53 A B C D E	78 A B C D E	103 A B C D E
4 A B C D E	29 A B C D E	54 A B C D E	79 A B C D E	104 A B C D E
5 A B C D E	30 A B C D E	55 A B C D E	80 A B C D E	105 A B C D E
6 A B C D E	31 A B C D E	56 A B C D E	81 A B C D E	106 A B C D E
7 A B C D E	32 A B C D E	57 A B C D E	82 A B C D E	107 A B C D E
8 A B C D E	33 A B C D E	58 A B C D E	83 A B C D E	108 A B C D E
9 A B C D E	34 A B C D E	59 A B C D E	84 A B C D E	109 A B C D E
10 A B C D E	35 A B C D E	60 A B C D E	85 A B C D E	110 A B C D E

Make only ONE mark for each answer. Additional and stray marks may be counted as mistakes. In making corrections, erase errors COMPLETELY.

11 A B C D E	36 A B C D E	61 A B C D E	86 A B C D E	111 A B C D E
12 A B C D E	37 A B C D E	62 A B C D E	87 A B C D E	112 A B C D E
13 A B C D E	38 A B C D E	63 A B C D E	88 A B C D E	113 A B C D E
14 A B C D E	39 A B C D E	64 A B C D E	89 A B C D E	114 A B C D E
15 A B C D E	40 A B C D E	65 A B C D E	90 A B C D E	115 A B C D E
16 A B C D E	41 A B C D E	66 A B C D E	91 A B C D E	116 A B C D E
17 A B C D E	42 A B C D E	67 A B C D E	92 A B C D E	117 A B C D E
18 A B C D E	43 A B C D E	68 A B C D E	93 A B C D E	118 A B C D E
19 A B C D E	44 A B C D E	69 A B C D E	94 A B C D E	119 A B C D E
20 A B C D E	45 A B C D E	70 A B C D E	95 A B C D E	120 A B C D E
21 A B C D E	46 A B C D E	71 A B C D E	96 A B C D E	121 A B C D E
22 A B C D E	47 A B C D E	72 A B C D E	97 A B C D E	122 A B C D E
23 A B C D E	48 A B C D E	73 A B C D E	98 A B C D E	123 A B C D E
24 A B C D E	49 A B C D E	74 A B C D E	99 A B C D E	124 A B C D E
25 A B C D E	50 A B C D E	75 A B C D E	100 A B C D E	125 A B C D E

ANSWER SHEET

DEC - - 2016

TEST NO. _____ PART ____ TITLE OF POSITION _____
(AS GIVEN IN EXAMINATION ANNOUNCEMENT - INCLUDE OPTION, IF ANY)

PLACE OF EXAMINATION _____ DATE _____
(CITY OR TOWN)   (STATE)

RATING

USE THE SPECIAL PENCIL.   MAKE GLOSSY BLACK MARKS.

Make only ONE mark for each answer. Additional and stray marks may be counted as mistakes. In making corrections, erase errors COMPLETELY.